Teaching, Learni..
Research in Higher Edt RARY

Teaching, Learning and Research in Higher Education offers a combination of critical perspectives and practical advice that is ideally suited for individuals interested in enhancing their practice through analysis and critique. The aim is to promote a critical understanding of one's own practices: to foster personal and professional formation through a reflexive engagement with one's environment and circumstances. At a practical level this means continuously thinking about how to adjust practice rather than following a formulaic approach derived from any particular educational theory.

Teaching, Learning and Research in Higher Education argues that academics can find space for their own agency in the midst of institutional policies and practices that serve to frame, as well as delimit and constrain, what counts as good academic work in teaching and research. This text bridges a gap between those books that provide a high-level analysis of contemporary higher education, the more practical texts on how to be a good teacher in higher education and those texts which aim to improve teaching through a better understanding of the learning process.

Topical chapters include:

> Framing Teacher–Learner Relationships, Learning Groups, Teaching for Diversity, Assessment, Promoting Workplace-Oriented Learning, Learning in the Digital Age and Teaching and Research.

A must-have resource for higher education professions, academic developers, professionals and anyone looking to improve their teaching and learning practices, *Teaching, Learning and Research in Higher Education* is also appropriate for continuing and professional development courses in the UK and teaching and learning courses in the US.

Mark Tennant is Professor of Education and Dean of the University Graduate School, University of Technology, Sydney.

Cathi McMullen is Senior Lecturer in the School of Marketing and Management at Charles Sturt University, Australia.

Dan Kaczynski is Professor in the Educational Leadership department at Central Michigan University.

Teaching, Learning and Research in Higher Education

A Critical Approach

Mark Tennant, Cathi McMullen and Dan Kaczynski

Routledge
Taylor & Francis Group

NEW YORK AND LONDON

First published 2010
by Routledge
270 Madison Ave, New York, NY 10016

Simultaneously published in the UK
by Routledge
2 Park Square, Milton Park, Abingdon, Oxon OX14 4RN

Routledge is an imprint of the Taylor & Francis Group, an informa business

© 2010 Taylor & Francis

Typeset in Minion by
RefineCatch Limited, Bungay, Suffolk
Printed and bound in the United States of America on acid-free paper by
Walsworth Publishing Company, Marceline, MO

Library of Congress Cataloging in Publication Data
Tennant, Mark.
    Teaching, learning and research in higher education : a critical approach / by Mark Tennant, Cathi
    McMullen, and Dan Kaczynski.
        p. cm.
    College teaching. 2. College teachers—Professional relationships. I. McMullen, Cathi. II. Kaczynski,
    Dan. III. Title.
    LB2331.T4295 2009
    378.1'25—dc22
    2008054227

ISBN 10: 0–415–96272–2 (hbk)
ISBN 10: 0–415–96263–3 (pbk)
ISBN 10: 0–203–87591–5 (ebk)

ISBN 13: 978–0–415–96272–8 (hbk)
ISBN 13: 978–0–415–96263–6 (pbk)
ISBN 13: 978–0–203–87591–9 (ebk)

Contents

Illustrations

Figures

Tables

Preface

This book is designed to fill what we see as a gap in the literature, between those books that provide a high-level analysis and theoretical treatment of contemporary higher education (e.g. Barnett, 2005 or Gibbons, Limoges, Nowotny et al., 1994) and the more practically focused texts on how to be a good teacher in higher education (e.g. Fry, Ketteridge & Marshall, 2003). Throughout we draw on both the literature on higher education and our collective practical experience in teaching, management and research.

The overall aim of the book is to provide a critical and practical perspective on teaching, learning and research in higher education and to foster a more reflexive engagement with issues at the systemic, institutional and personal levels. For academics in particular the aim is to promote a critical understanding of their own developing practices and how they position themselves as workers in contemporary academic life. At a practical level this means continuously thinking about and adjusting everyday professional practices rather than following a formulaic approach derived from any particular educational theory.

Each chapter has a section at the end titled 'Enhancing Professional Practice', the aim of which is to provide the reader with an activity to bring out the practical implications of the material.

The book commences with an analysis of the work context of the contemporary academic. As we write there are some significant contemporary events unfolding which will no doubt have an impact on the future shape of higher education. For example, the global financial and economic crisis is yet to have its full impact, but already many universities have had huge reductions in the value of their endowment and investment funds, the most dramatic example is Harvard University which has had the value of its endowment reduced by $US 4.5 billion (Jan, 2008). Governments too have indicated their intention to reduce funding for public universities (e.g. the states of California and New York), and no doubt there will be a reduced capacity to pay for university fees both domestically and internationally. Much is made in the book about the trend towards the marketisation of higher education – it may be that a long-term outcome of the economic downturn is a move away from the market in advanced western economies and a corresponding return to earlier relationships between universities, the state and business. Of course some eminent people in the higher education sector believe that universities are still overly used as vehicles to deliver the social and economic policies of government. For example, Chris Patten, the Vice-Chancellor of Oxford University recently asserted that universities should not have a social security function:

> The debate on widening participation in Britain's universities heated up last week with the publication of a report on special schemes to encourage pupils from poorer backgrounds to enter higher education, and inflammatory remarks by the Chancellor of Oxford University. Lord (Chris) Patten told a conference of independent school heads that his university should not be treated "like a social security office" to help disadvantaged pupils from state schools.
>
> (Spencer, 2008)

Debates about the role of the university and its relationship with the state, economic life, business, industry and the community are very much alive and present in the working lives of academics. They are played out in the formulation of student rules, curriculum practices and ongoing policy discussions within universities. And they are played out in the three core functions of a university and their relationship: teaching, research and community and professional service.

In the opening chapter some of the key trends in contemporary academic life are highlighted such as:

- The shift from individual to team-based academic work
- The corporatisation and privatisation of universities
- The increasing demand for knowledge to be 'useful'
- The development of a global education 'market'
- The production of 'new economy' workers, including academics as 'knowledge workers'
- A growing emphasis on quality assurance and accountability
- Shifting relationships with 'the workplace'

- The impact of information and communication technologies
- Growth and diversity in the student population.

Chapter 2 'Perspectives on Quality Teaching' focuses on the system-wide and institutional shaping of what it means to be a good or expert teacher and what it means to provide a 'quality' teaching programme. It analyses different conceptual approaches to what constitutes good teaching, and the way in which systemic and localised student surveys frame our understanding of good teaching.

Chapter 3 'Reconceptualising the Development of University Teaching Expertise' follows on from the quality issues raised in the immediately preceding chapter. While Chapter 2 partly deconstructs the assumptions underlying the way in which 'good teaching' is framed, Chapter 3 addresses the issue of how academics can develop and sustain their expertise as teachers. In so doing it draws together the concepts of teaching expertise and teacher identities.

The aim of Chapter 4 'Framing Teacher–Learner Relationships' is to surface and analyse the variety of ways in which teachers position themselves or are positioned as authority figures and 'knowers' in the academic context. It explores the philosophical, educational and psychological dimensions of the teacher–learner relationship and how different institutional and pedagogical practices position teachers in different ways.

Learning groups are the focus of Chapter 5, which looks at the different ways in which groups have been used to foster learning in higher education. It will analyse the different group dynamics produced in different approaches to using groups (e.g. group discussions, group exercises, group tasks, simulations and games). It will then explore the implications for facilitating groups for learning.

Chapter 6 'Teaching for Diversity' examines the implications of diversity and internationalisation for the work practices of academics in the higher education sector. It has two emphases: teaching to promote an awareness of diversity among students, and developing the capacity to teach an increasingly diverse student population comprising international students, minorities, older students and students with a disability.

Chapter 7, 'Assessment', explores two key tensions around assessment that institutions and academics negotiate on an ongoing basis. The first of these – the tension between assessment for certification and assessment for learning – impacts on considerations in regard to individual vs group learning, the role of feedback and the acquisition of knowledge and skill vs the acquisition of dispositions and attributes. The second of these tensions is between assessing academic as opposed to workplace or everyday problems – the latter drawing attention to the role of context, the availability (or not) of complete information and the merits of team problem solving. A key theme throughout is how the assessment regime shapes the teacher–learner relationship and how learners understand what is legitimate and important.

Our interest in Chapter 8 is in how the changing nature of education and its interface with the workplace produces, presupposes or otherwise shapes new learner identities and pedagogical practices. We also explore how engagement with the workplace has led to a challenge to the traditional disciplines, partly because workplace problems are not neatly packaged into disciplinary areas, and partly because knowledge is increasingly seen as being 'produced' in the workplace.

The aim of Chapter 9 'Learning in the Digital Age' is to analyse the way in which technology-enhanced learning changes both the group dynamics and the nature of the teacher–learner relationship. It also looks at the new kinds of academic work practices promoted by technology.

In Chapter 10 'Postgraduate Research Education' a range of issues are analysed relating to the supervision of research students and research education more broadly. Issues include:

- The dynamics of the supervisory relationship
- The development of generic skills
- Embedding students in a research culture
- System-wide measures of quality of research education
- The focus on outcomes – especially relating to employment and the exploitation of intellectual property.

Finally, the relationship between teaching and research is examined in Chapter 11. This chapter analyses the debate concerning the relationship between teaching and research. It particularly looks at the scholarship of teaching and the idea of research-led teaching. It examines the possibilities of teachers researching their practice and of using research as a learning tool for students.

We would like to acknowledge that Chapter 5 'Learning Groups' is a reworked version of Chapter 8 in Tennant, M. (2006) *Psychology and adult learning* (3rd ed.). London: Routledge. Some material in Chapter 8 'Promoting Workplace-Oriented Learning' has appeared in Tennant, M. (2000) Learning to work, working to learn: Theories of situational education. In C. Symes and J. McIntyre (Eds.), *Working knowledge: The new vocationalism and higher education*. Milton Keynes: Open University Press, 123–134; and in M. Tennant (2005) Transforming selves. *Journal of Transformative Education*, 3(2), 102–115. Finally, some material from Chapter 10 'Postgraduate Research Education' appears in Boud, D. and Tennant, M. (2006) Putting doctoral education to work: Challenges to academic practice.

Higher Education Research and Development, 25(3), 309–322; Tennant, M. (2009) Regulatory regimes in doctoral education. In D. Boud and A. Lee (Eds.), *Changing practices of doctoral education.* London: Routledge, 226–235; and in Tennant, M. and Roberts, S. (2007) Agreeing to supervise. In C. Denholm and T. Evans (Eds.), *Supervising doctorates downunder: Keys to effective supervision in Australia and New Zealand.* Melbourne: ACER Press, 20–27.

All teacher interviews (Carolyn, David, John, Joy and Sandra) are taken from McMullen, C. (2008) Developing and sustaining university teaching expertise in times of change: A narrative study with award winning university teachers. Doctoral dissertation, University of Technology, Sydney.

Finally we would like to acknowledge all those who have enriched our working lives as academics in higher education.

Mark Tennant
Cathi McMullen
Dan Kaczynski

CHAPTER 1

Introduction

The overarching argument of this book is that academics can find space for their own agency in the midst of system-wide and institutional policies and practices that serve to frame, as well as delimit and constrain, what counts as good academic work in teaching and research. We argue that academics can develop a sense of agency through a reflexive engagement with the circumstances in which they find themselves. How do the various systemic, institutional and personal circumstances present themselves? What do they say about who you should 'be' as an academic? Is there a single uniform voice on how to be? Arguably, such questions are necessary starting points for developing a critical understanding of your own developing practices and how you position yourself as a worker in contemporary academic life. And so we commence with an exploration of some of the forces and trends at play in higher education in the past few decades.

It is possible to characterise these trends in a variety of ways, but there are some key features that lie at their heart: the growth of participation in higher education worldwide, the increasing diversity of the student population, the transforming effect of information and communication technologies, the demand from stakeholders that education be relevant to working life, the growing global competition in the production and distribution of knowledge and the renewed concern with accountability, standards and quality assurance.

As a result the university sector has been transformed with contemporary academic workplaces characterised by ongoing change, complexity and diversity. Universities are now very different places from the universities where current academics studied as students and perhaps began their teaching and research careers. This has had a significant impact on the practices and identities of university teachers and their students.

Our aim in this chapter is to present a broad overview of some of the changes in the higher education sector and the impact these changes have had and will continue to have on university work. While these changes have brought benefits, such as greater attention to the quality of teaching, greater access to university education and the benefits of electronic communication (Anderson, Johnson & Saha, 2002), they have presented many challenges to those working in the sector.

Growth and Diversity

The second half of the 20th century was characterised by a move towards mass higher education. The Organisation for Economic Co-operation and Development (OECD) estimates there are now around 132 million students enrolled in tertiary education globally, up from 68 million in 1991 ('tertiary education' here includes community and technical colleges). This constitutes an average growth of over 5% per year over the period of 1991 to 2004 (Nuthall, 2008).

There has been growth in the participation of women, different ethnic groups and older adults, together with growth in international student enrolments. It is likely that the student population in higher education will continue to become more diverse given that the participation of non-traditional groups remains lower than for other groups, and that international student numbers are predicted to grow.

This combination of rising student numbers, rising student–staff ratios and a more diverse student body has presented new challenges for university teachers. New kinds of students are often less prepared for traditional styles of university study – they may ask different questions, have different perspectives on issues, react differently to group exercises and generally bring different experiences to the classroom. This may not, or should not, be a problem, but it is a challenge because teachers can no longer rely on the assumptions they may have held for more homogenous groups. Some of these challenges are explored in Chapter 6.

The Marketisation of Higher Education and Global Competition

Universities are more than ever positioned as important sites for the production and dissemination of knowledge and innovation in the service of national economic prosperity. As such they are becoming more corporate in their outlook, which stands in contrast to the values of collegial decision-making. Naidoo (2005) neatly captures this trend:

> Governments world-wide have begun to implement funding and governance frameworks based on market principles ... there has been a global trend away from forms of funding and regulation which were based on Keynesian welfare principles and the 'social compact' that evolved between higher education, the state and society over the last century ... In addition, management principles derived from the private sector which monitor, measure, compare and judge professional activities have been applied in the hope that the functioning of higher education will be enhanced. Such mechanisms are also expected to aid consumer choice. (pp. 27–28)

She argues that rather than providing student empowerment, student choice, equity, efficiency and higher quality, the trend towards market forces results instead in the commodification of higher education, which ultimately deters innovation and promotes passive and instrumental attitudes among students and researchers. Thus students are reconfigured as 'consumers' of educational 'product' and research is valued according to its capacity to generate income. Whether one agrees with her argument in its entirety or not, it is fair to say that most academics have experienced this shift in their working lives.

This trend towards the market has a global dimension as nation states, and the universities within them, are increasingly operating and being evaluated in a global marketplace. Testimony to this is the growing significance and impact of world league tables. There have already been two significant studies of the impact of the world leagues tables, one conducted by the OECD and the other by the Higher Education Funding Council for England. The OECD paper (2007) points out that there are approximately 17,000 higher education institutions around the globe but that there seems to be almost an obsession with the status and trajectory of the top 100. Hazelkorn (2007) remarks:

> Over recent decades, rankings or 'league tables' have become a feature of many countries. They are usually published by government and accreditation agencies, higher education, research and commercial organisations or the popular media.
>
> As higher education has become globalised and internationalised, worldwide rankings have appeared, such as the Shanghai Jiao Tong list and that produced by the THES. The former has effectively become the brand leader, regularly referenced by university leaders and government ministers.

The OECD survey of senior managers in 202 higher education institutions across 41 countries revealed that:

- 58% of respondents were not happy with their current ranking
- 70% want to be in the top 10% nationally
- 71% want to be in the top 25% internationally
- 57% believe league tables and rankings are influencing the willingness of other institutions to form partnerships with them
- 56% have a formal internal mechanism for reviewing their rank order.

What impact can world rankings have on academics working in a discipline or field of study within their university? The answer to this can be found in the way in which national governments and individual higher education institutions have responded to the rankings. Hazelkorn found that nearly all the universities who participated in the survey have taken internal steps to improve their ranking.

> The majority have a formal process to review the results, usually by the president/rector, and are taking strategic, organisational, managerial and/or academic actions. These include embedding rankings in strategic decision-making processes and 'target agreements' with faculties, establishing a 'new section to monitor rankings', 'developing better management tools', and providing 'more scholarships and staff appointments'.

Hazelkorn also points out that the excellence initiatives in Germany, Russia, China and France are directly related to the rankings process. The European Union is now planning to develop its own international university ranking system (Marshall, 2008). The point is that academics cannot isolate themselves from how the world defines and constrains what it means to be an excellent university and by implication, what it means to be an excellent academic. At the very least they need to engage in this debate as it is increasingly being shaped by the metrics used in world and national rankings.

Uniformity of Systems and Processes

The drive to establish more uniform systems and processes in higher education is partly a risk management response to growth and diversity in the sector, and partly a response to the increasing demands for the mobility of qualifications, students and staff. This is well illustrated by the European initiative known as the Bologna process, which aims to establish, by 2010, a European Higher Education Area among the 46 signatory nations. The idea is to have a uniform degree structure comprising undergraduate level study (3 years), masters level study (2 years) and doctoral study (3 years). This is combined with a common credit point system (60 credits for one full-time year of study) and a Diploma Supplement which is a uniform and consistent method of describing the nature, level, context, content and status of studies. Finally there are to be quality assurance systems at institutional, national and European levels. This is all in the interests of the mutual recognition of qualifications and the adoption of common standards in order both to promote the mobility, across borders, of students and staff working in the higher education sector, and to provide employers and the public generally with a common understanding of what a degree in a particular area means. Philip Fine, writing in *University World News* (2008), points to the universal interest in the Bologna process:

> The Bologna process, the initiative that tries to smooth the jagged edges off Europe's differing degree and credit structure, has caught the world's attention in a big way. From the Caribbean to Canada, from China to Australia, the plan designed to solve a European problem and that then brought in bordering countries now has nations far beyond those borders looking at some academic retooling.

But the system described above does not accord very well with the preference in North America for four-year undergraduate degrees or with some pathways in Australia which follow the four-year undergraduate degree with a one-year Masters. It also does not accord very well with the honours year added onto many Australian three-year degrees. There is evidence that some Asian countries are looking to align with the Bologna model but Singapore, China and Hong Kong are increasingly favouring the North American structure. And so there is evidence of resistance to the Bologna model in the US and Asia and even within Europe. However, the US itself is taking notice of the Bologna model, with a recent report from the Institute for Higher Education Policy in Washington (Adelman, 2008) stating that 'it has sufficient momentum to become the dominant global higher education model within the next two decades' (p. 2) – the Report itself recommends a number of initiatives in response to the European reforms, including the development of a qualifications framework for state higher education institutions and the development of a US version of the Diploma Supplement. The prevailing question for universities outside Europe and North America is whether to align with one or the other of these structures, or to not align at all. The problem with the latter is that a lack of alignment will be an impediment to the mobility of students in study abroad schemes. It will also cause uncertainty about the acceptability of overseas qualifications for the purposes of employment or further higher degree study, and a potential erosion of international student demand. Once again such initiatives eventually embroil individual academics as they engage in internal institutional debates about credit points, the length of degrees and the value of generic statements of attainment such as the Diploma Supplement.

Internationalisation

Internationalisation has emerged as a strategic goal for many universities. Internationalisation normally refers to two things; first, the opening up of universities to international students; and, second, the need for universities to develop a genuinely international curriculum focus in order to prepare students to work in the global labour market. A recent OECD report (2007) shows that the number of students studying outside their own country is more than 2.7 million globally, which is a fourfold increase over the last three decades (OECD by UNESCO's Institute for Statistics). The US has long been the top destination for overseas students but its market share is falling, while it has been growing in Australia, France, Japan and New Zealand. The US has nearly twice the number of international students that Britain has, its nearest rival (at 12% share), followed by Germany (10%), France (9%), Australia (6%) and then Japan (5%). Australia has the highest percentage of international students as a percentage of its overall enrolment (17%) while the OECD average is only 6.7%.

There are many advantages to having a large international cohort of students – they bring fees to the institution, they help to promote an international outlook among the domestic students, they may form connections at university which are later transformed into business or other collaborations. Most of the concerns about international students have to do with their literacy levels in the host country (predominantly English), their employability, their need for additional support, the potential lowering of admission and assessment standards and the 'replacement' of domestic student places with international student places. While a large cohort of international students puts pressure on universities and individual academics, it also highlights the need for academics to adapt to people from different backgrounds who have different values and ways of being in the world – which also applies where there are a large cohort of 'non-traditional' domestic students.

Finally, the internationalisation of the curriculum is a goal adopted by many universities but its realisation in practice is subtle and difficult. It is often addressed by a period of 'study abroad' without any connection back to the domestic curriculum upon return. Many academics feel that knowledge is global and therefore nothing really has to be done in this area.

However, while this may be true in areas such as pure mathematics and physics, in most areas of study the questions that are asked, the knowledge being generated and the teaching approaches adopted are often linked to specific social and historical contexts. Moving beyond these contexts is a significant challenge for academics working in a globally focused university.

Information and Communication Technologies

Information and communication technologies are also transforming academic workplaces and the experiences of students, allowing new possibilities for online research collaborations, global online networking and, perhaps most significantly, the online delivery of content. The New Media Consortium in its annual Horizon Report (2008) points to the key contemporary technologies likely to shape the future of learning and teaching. Two examples are 'grassroots video' and 'collaboration webs'. Grassroots video refers to the widespread production and dissemination of video content through hosting services like YouTube and iTunes. The ease of video production and dissemination through inexpensive everyday devices allows more possibilities for teachers to use video for teaching, assignments, data collection and assessment. The second example is 'collaboration webs', which refers to the ever-increasing availability of web-based tools, infrastructure and applications that allow for collaborative work among those who are geographically separated:

> The essential attribute of the technologies in this set is that they make it easy for people to share interests and ideas, work on joint projects, and easily monitor collective progress. All of these are needs common to student work, research, collaborative teaching, writing and authoring, development of grant proposals, and more. Using them, groups can collaborate on projects online, anywhere there is Internet access; interim results of research can be shared among a team, supporting illustrations and tables created, and all changes and iterations tracked, documented, and archived. In class situations, faculty can evaluate student work as it progresses, leaving detailed comments right in the documents if desired in almost real time. Students can work with other students in distant locations, or with faculty as they engage in fieldwork. (p. 14)

While the possibilities are exciting, they also bring challenges to our traditional understandings of teaching and research: the 'classroom' necessarily becomes more public and interactive, with new patterns of participation among students, new ways of engaging with the material and new sets of relationships between teachers and students. An example of the latter is the increased one-to-one contact between students and teachers through email or online sites. The downside of this increased communication is the way in which it impacts academic workloads. In their study titled, *Changes in academic work*, Anderson, Johnson and Saha (2002) found a near unanimous view that dealing responsibly with students' emails takes a large amount of time, more time than student contact in the pre-electronic era. The impact of information and communication technologies (ICTs) on teaching and learning in higher education is the focus of Chapter 9.

New Conceptions of Knowledge

Formal educational institutions are under scrutiny to provide education that is more 'relevant', that is, pertinent to the needs of employers, which often means learning which is less abstract and discipline-bound and closer to the problems and issues found in work contexts. There is an ever-increasing call for teaching and research to address the urgent problems presented in working and social life. Because these problems typically cut across disciplinary boundaries, interdisciplinary approaches are needed. This requires quite a perspective shift in thinking about the activities of teaching and research given that they are historically located within disciplinary paradigms. A disciplinary approach is cumulative in the sense that it adds to the stock of knowledge, and progressive in that it moves inexorably towards better solutions. By contrast, an interdisciplinary approach crosses disciplinary and theoretical domains and learning fields. It argues that a single disciplinary focus does not engage in the complexities of contemporary work and lives. It aims to integrate perspectives from multiple disciplines so that conventional boundaries are transcended and new ways of thinking become possible (Solomon, 2008). This issue is addressed partly in the chapter on workplace learning (Chapter 8) and partly in the chapter on teaching and research (Chapter 11).

Accountability and Quality Assurance

Higher education has been increasingly viewed as an economic resource that should be organised to maximise its contribution to economic development. This has been accompanied by increasing demands for accountability from stakeholders – universities are seen as having a responsibility to society, which expects something in return for the public investment provided for them.

The US, for example, is pursuing a renewed agenda focusing on accountability and quality assurance. Testimony to this is the recent report (2006) commissioned by the US Secretary of Education, Margaret Spellings on the future of US higher education. The Report outlines the perceived deficiencies and threats to US higher education, stating quite unequivocally the kind of higher education needed:

- We want a world-class higher-education system that creates new knowledge, contributes to economic prosperity and global competitiveness, and empowers citizens
- We want a system that is accessible to all Americans, throughout their lives
- We want postsecondary institutions to provide high-quality instruction while improving their efficiency in order to be more affordable to the students, taxpayers, and donors who sustain them
- We want a higher-education system that gives Americans the workplace skills they need to adapt to a rapidly changing economy
- We want postsecondary institutions to adapt to a world altered by technology, demographics and globalization, in which the higher-education landscape includes new providers and new paradigms, from for-profit universities to distance learning. (Spellings, 2006, p. vii)

The above vision captures quite nicely the way in which key issues are being configured in universities around the world: the need for nations to be globally competitive, the need to make education accessible to all, the need to improve efficiencies, the need to cater for the demands of the contemporary workforce and the need to embrace new technologies and new and innovative paradigms for teaching and research. In this context the Spellings' Report focuses on the need for public accountability for the performance of universities and their teachers. Its vision for US higher education is the widespread adoption of a culture of continuous innovation and quality improvement. This includes the public reporting of student achievement and common comprehensive datasets which allow for comparisons between institutions. The public policy instruments used to achieve this include incentive schemes such as matching funding for complying institutions, and the need to include public accountability within accreditation regimes.

The move towards more accountability and stronger quality assurance processes is a feature of universities worldwide and reflects a shifting relationship between governments and universities, although from vastly different starting points. In Australia, for example, the reconstruction of universities formed part of a larger reconstruction of the public sector (Marginson, 1995). From the mid 1980s onwards the Australian

Government embraced 'marketisation' and higher education policy became directed by faith in the markets and a business model of higher education. Market competition via tuition fees, industry funding, international marketing and private universities was seen as a way to produce a more efficient system. Effectively, in the shift to enterprise, the Australian Government has repositioned itself from being a patron of universities to a purchaser of higher education expecting demonstrated accountability and return for this investment (Coaldrake & Stedman, 1999). This shift is also apparent in other countries where the government has had a history of providing higher education.

The impact of quality assurance on the teaching role of academics is taken up in Chapter 2, which looks at the way in which regimes of teacher evaluation frame what it means to be a good teacher. The argument in this chapter is that good teaching must be demonstrated in relation to institutionally defined criteria in what has been referred to as a 'performative' culture:

> Performativity . . . requires individual practitioners to organize themselves as a response to targets, indicators and evaluations. To set aside personal beliefs and commitments and live an existence of calculation. The new performative worker is a promiscuous self, an enterprising self, with a passion for excellence. For some, this is an opportunity to make a success of themselves, for others it portends inner conflicts, inauthenticity and resistance. It is also suggested that performativity produces opacity rather than transparency as individuals and organizations take ever greater care in the construction and maintenance of fabrications.
>
> (Ball, 2003, p. 215)

Ball argues that as education reform spreads across the globe it is becoming thoroughly embedded in the 'assumptive worlds' of many academic educators. This reform does not simply change what people as educators, scholars and researchers do; it changes who they are. In similar vein, Nixon (1996) comments that the reorganisation of higher education policy, structures and practices during the 1990s has impacted on the professional roles, identities, wellbeing and productivity of those who teach in universities.

Perhaps the most significant impact on the identity of the academic is the shift from what may be described as 'the academic as independent, autonomous professional working within a disciplinary area in a collegial environment' to the 'academic as corporate employee delivering high quality product to the market'. This shift is accompanied by a new set of demands being placed on academics: they need to work in different ways with students and administrative support staff, they need to develop new relationships with external agencies, they need to contribute to the corporate culture of the university and they need to develop their own capabilities in areas related to the strategic interests of the university (e.g. budgeting skills, advertising, marketing, negotiating contracts, public relations, networking, teamwork, self-appraisal). In this changed and changing university environment, university teachers face multiple challenges. Coaldrake and Stedman (1999) identify five main areas where the effects of change on academic work can be observed. These are:

- Growing pressures on time, workload and morale
- Increased emphasis on performance, professional standards and accountability
- A shift in staffing policies from local control and individual autonomy to a more collective and institutional focus
- Academic work becoming more specialised and complex
- Diffusion and blurring of roles.

With the 'enterprise' university presenting new and varied demands on university teachers, conceptions of teaching expertise and teacher identity as stable and enduring are no longer sustainable. In these times of complexity and uncertainty in universities when academic identities are being challenged, competing views emerge about what it means to be an expert teacher. Developing teaching expertise is not simply a matter of acquiring new skills and knowledge – it is about taking up new identities, new ways of understanding and conducting oneself (see Chapter 3). This necessarily entails a reflexive engagement with work.

By a 'reflexive engagement with work' we mean understanding oneself and critically evaluating your 'working self', the circumstances in which you work and the way you are positioned in your work relationships. Of course such a posture is likely to be a general feature of your approach to family, institutional and community life. It is also likely to be a feature of your approach to teaching, which will be evident in two ways: first, in an ongoing reflexive engagement with your teaching practices, and, second, in providing students with the wherewithal to engage reflexively with *their* work (actual or anticipated). From a pedagogical point of view then, a reflexive approach means providing learning experiences that engage students in the uncertainties, messiness and value conflicts of 'real world' problems. There is evidence that curricula are changing in this way with workplace experiences, portfolio development, reflective journals, work based projects, action research, community-based projects and so on all well established at different levels of education. The kinds of tasks that students now undertake provide scope both for engagement with the world and for reflecting on and acting upon themselves. Of course the different pedagogical designs that invite students to act upon themselves in various ways do not guarantee that students will develop the capacity for 'reflexive engagement' as we have described it. Promoting a 'critical' engagement is the key – which allows the possibility of questioning existing practices rather than simply aligning oneself with institutional priorities, goals, visions and ways of doing things. This book encourages a reflexive approach, not only as an approach to teaching, but as an approach to working life as an academic in higher education.

CHAPTER 2

Perspectives on Quality Teaching

Where do we get our ideas about what constitutes good teaching? There are clearly many sources for our ideas: our own experience as learners, our experience of 'what works', observing and talking with colleagues, public debate about education and scholarly research and writing on education. Our developing ideas of good teaching, however, always occur within a broader context and they come up against institutionally endorsed notions of what education should be about and how we should measure and prove the value of our teaching. Institutions, in turn, live in a broader political and social context which demands certain things from them – for example that graduates are prepared for the workplace, that they are articulate and good communicators, that they have high levels of technical skill and that they can work well in teams (amongst a host of other attributes). And certain things are demanded of teachers in universities – that they are well prepared, up to date and well qualified, that they design appropriate assessments, provide good feedback to students, adapt materials and activities to suit the needs and capacities of students and so on. Such demands typically find expression in the call for universities and teachers to be more accountable for their actions and outputs. Thus we see a more concerted effort by governments, accreditation agencies and/or peak bodies to regulate and control universities, largely through more rigorous accreditation provisions, audit mechanisms, and requirements relating to standards and quality assurance processes. Indeed, universities themselves have moved to intensify central regulation and control over the activities of departments and schools. Typically, universities have set targets or key performance indicators for teaching that they strive to meet. These relate to areas such as student demand, retention, completions, equity, diversity and, of course, student evaluations of courses. One aspect of this regulation and control is the measurement of teaching performance, both at the level of the individual teacher, the course, and at the level of the institution as a whole. It is clear, however, that different student evaluation questionnaires contain within them implicit assumptions about what constitutes good teaching. This is the point of departure for this chapter which, in part, analyses the assumptions underlying different kinds of evaluation instruments. These assumptions, and the practices and discourses they promote, often have their origins in wider public and scholarly debate about the purposes and goals of education and the nature of learning. Our argument is that, as teachers, we need to be aware of the way in which our conceptions of teaching and our identity as teachers is shaped by such discourses and practices. Additionally we understand 'good teaching' to be a highly contested notion, and as such we need to adopt a critical approach to any instrument that serves to delimit and frame what it means to be a 'good teacher'. For this reason we commence with a brief exploration of some views on the goals and purposes of education and the nature of learning. These have their basis in scholarly empirical and theoretical work, but for the purposes of this chapter they are treated, not as theoretical positions to be analysed, but as discourses that have found their way into the everyday work practices of teachers. There are many ways to categorise such discourses, but perhaps the best for the current purpose is provided by Skelton (2005), who identifies four discourses: the traditional liberal, the psychologised, the performative and the critical. He used these categories for the purpose of analysing the practices of higher education teachers who have received teaching awards in the UK. Although we use the same categories we provide a different take on them.

Traditional Liberal

If we think of traditional university education as being in the liberal tradition, then education is said to lead to a greater awareness of self through cultivating an identity which is independent, rational, autonomous, coherent and which has a sense of social responsibility. The good learner is one who, with proper guidance, is brought to apprehend:

> the great outlines of knowledge, the principles on which it rests, the scale of its parts, its lights and shades . . . hence it is that his education is called 'Liberal'. A habit of mind is formed which lasts through life, of which the attributes are freedom, equitableness, calmness, moderation and wisdom . . .
>
> (Newman, 1999, p. 93)

On this account the subject of pedagogy is the production of a singular ideal type: the 'educated person', towards which one progressively develops through disciplined study and engagement in rational argument. The hallmark of a liberal education is the acquisition of universal and timeless knowledge that transcends the mundane needs of everyday life. It is education for its own sake – a quest for knowledge for what it is rather than for what it does. There is thus an emphasis on general education, accumulated wisdom and classic texts. There is a corresponding valuing of thought over action, and the contemplative life over a life devoted to a vocation. Even though there was a general aversion to vocational education, in reality, as Symes (2000) points out, there was an indirect vocational outcome from such an education:

> Even though liberal education was closely linked to the cultural needs of the leisured class which, by dint of is social rank and pecuniary means, was liberated from the need to obtain employment, in reality, many members of this class did so . . . This was certainly the case in the nineteenth century, when a university education was a vehicle for securing a position in civil administration or the church. A university education provided a particular kind of self-formation . . . upon which the workings of the church and government were said to be dependent. (p. 35)

While a liberal education as portrayed above does not seem pertinent to the contemporary world, elements of the liberal approach persist in educational discourse. For example, the argument that a liberal curriculum promotes the development of broader generic capacities and thinking skills that can be applied across a range of contexts, as opposed to a more instrumental education that is narrower, more specialised and more quickly outmoded. The liberal education legacy today can be found in ongoing debates in universities concerning the right balance between general and specialised aspects of the curriculum.

As far as good teaching is concerned, within the liberal approach the needs, interests, motivations and capacities of students are assumed and therefore do not figure in the pedagogical space. Nor do teachers need to be concerned with the application of knowledge to professional practice or with tapping into the experiences of students. The main thing that is expected of teachers is that they have mastery of their discipline and a capacity to provide a clear exposition of disciplinary knowledge – normally in the form of a lecture. Students for their part are expected to acquire disciplinary knowledge and develop a capacity to think logically and critically about the subject matter. Student evaluations of teaching are not really a part of the liberal tradition where disciplinary and pedagogical authority is vested in the teacher and where students are not really seen as being in a position to make comments on the quality of their teachers.

Psychologised

Malcolm and Zukas (2001) use the term 'psychologised understandings of teaching' to refer to the way in which psychology has exerted its influence on our understandings of teaching and learning. They point out the way in which psychological terms and ideas have been dominant in educational discourse, especially in higher education. They argue that much of our understanding of teaching and learning in higher education is dominated by psychological versions of the learner and teacher, unlike other areas of education in which philosophical and sociological understandings provide competing discourses. The problem with this, they argue, is that 'scientific psychology', with its emphasis on prediction and control, reduces the educational enterprise to the management of techniques, processes and behaviours; and as such promotes a view of teaching as undemanding 'craft work'.

> The tautological claim, implicit or explicit in so much of the literature of HE teaching, that we 'teach in order to facilitate learning', isolates educational work from the contested social and philosophical space in which it occurs, and reduces teachers to technicians who apply rules formulated by others. Ultimately, this must impoverish both the curriculum and the institution of higher education. (p. 37)

In addition they rightly point out that the psychological approach focuses on qualities that learners 'have' such as personality, intelligence, learning styles, learning preferences and learning behaviours, as if these were stable characteristics that exist without reference to how they are embedded in a social, cultural and historical context.

Malcolm and Zukas (2001) can be criticised for adopting a caricatured version of 'mainstream psychology' which does not do justice to the variety of psychological approaches available. However, they are really only concerned with how the psychological approach finds expression in the literature used to inform higher education policy makers and practitioners in the area of academic staff development, and in this regard they rightly point out the absence of any reference to critical writing in higher education and to more recent work in the area of feminist and post-structural psychologies. Nevertheless the vastly different theoretical positions in psychology do need some acknowledgement in so far as they provide a contested discourse for understanding higher education; namely behaviourism, cognitive psychology and humanistic psychology.

The behavioural approach is summed up nicely by Pratt and Nesbit (2000):

> thirty years ago, education was dominated by a discourse of behavi-orism: learning was defined as a change in behavior; if it couldn't be observed, it was not important. Teaching was, primarily, a matter of identifying what was to be learned, arranging the conditions for that learning, and assessing whether it had been learned. The tools for this approach were well specified. The language was of instructional technology and a systems approach to education. Through task analysis we could discover what skills, knowledge, and attitudes were needed; through instructional design we could translate that into learning objectives; and by matching outcomes with objectives we would know whether teaching was successful. (p. 119)

The behavioural approach was closely associated with the competency based movement which sought to define learning in terms of the com-petencies which needed to be acquired for a particular task, occupation or profession. Such competencies were typically broken down into compon-ent parts and written in behavioural terms. They were also seen as generic and therefore capable of being applied across a variety of contexts and purposes. A good teacher on this account is one who has mastered all the competencies relevant to teaching.

The retreat from behaviourism came as a result of criticisms of the behaviourist approach: for example, that not all the behavioural indicators of competence can be specified in advance, that not all learning outcomes are specifiable in behavioural terms, that subjective outcomes cannot be captured as behavioural objectives and that unplanned or incidental learn-ing is not being acknowledged (see Tennant, 2006). Furthermore there was a general move in psychology towards a more holistic understanding of the person and a more contextualised understanding of psychological phe-nomena. This was given expression in teaching variously as a valuing of the learner's experience and needs (the hallmark of the humanistic approach), a recognition of the active role of the learner in constructing their know-ledge (the hallmark of the constructivist approach) and an appreciation of the role of context in learning (the hallmark of the situated learning approach).

The humanistic approach is most closely associated with the prevailing discourse of 'learner-centred' education. Humanistic psychology partly emerged as a protest against the scientific conception of the person that reduced the person to an object to be studied. Instead it emphasised the human qualities of the person such as personal freedom, choice and the validity of subjective experience. A feature then of the humanistic approach is a concern with the 'holistic' self where the cognitive and emotional dimensions of learning are given equal weight. Carl Rogers (1983) is typically credited with bringing the techniques, practices and thinking of humanistic psychology to bear upon educational debate. In Rogers' view the good teacher is a 'facilitator' of learning, which means having empathy with and trust in learners, being genuine with learners and being open, caring and non-judgemental. And so 'learner-centred' education is characterised by a focus on developing a good teacher–learner relationship in an attempt to understand and meet learners' needs. As Pratt and Nesbit (2000) comment:

> This was an important discursive shift ... Now content, and the specification of what was to be learned, was subordinate to the learner's experience and participation. ... Learners were to be involved in specifying what would be learned, how it would be learned, and what would be an appropriate indication of learning ... The learner's experience, as a form of foundational knowledge, replaced the teacher's expertise as the primary compass that guided learning. As a consequence, the primary role of teacher shifted from teacher-as-authority to teacher-as-facilitator. (p. 120)

Interestingly, a different kind of learner-centred approach can be found in the cognitive approach to learning. Like humanistic psychology, cognitive psychology was also a reaction to behaviourism, in that its re-emergence in the 1960s was made possible by the failure of behaviourism to translate mental constructs into behaviourist terms. One particular strand of cognitive psychology is associated with a constructivist discourse. Such a discourse regards learners as constructing their own cognitive maps, cognitive structures or schemas as a result of their experience. So, like the humanistic approach, individual experience is the building block for learning and the object of teaching is to help learners construct more integrated and general cognitive structures that can be applied across a range of contexts. Skelton (2005) comments:

> Methods that focus on the content of teaching and its transfer, such as the didactic lecture, are considered to have limited value since they fail to take into consideration the different ways in which individual learners make sense of and 'process' the material. 'Student-centred' approaches and 'constructivist' ideas and theories have become popular in the light of the critique of didactic teaching. They recognize that students actively construct meaning in the light of their existing knowledge and experiences. Constructivist theories maintain that teachers need to offer learning experiences that recognize and

extend the student's existing frame of reference and understanding. (p. 32)

Good teaching starts from where the students are at, and provides experiences to extend and deepen their understanding. A contemporary expression of this view that there are underlying cognitive structures that frame our understanding of the world can be found in the distinction between 'deep' and 'surface' learning, a distinction which is widely held and very persistent among those involved in teacher development in higher education. Yet this conception is profoundly challenged by theories of 'situated learning' and 'situated cognition' which hold that learning is more than the building of cognitive structures in isolation from practice – participation in a community of practice, with its social networks, roles and relationships is an integral part of learning. From this perspective it makes no sense to talk of knowledge that is decontextualised, abstract or general, and thus the distinction between 'deep' and 'surface' knowledge cannot be sustained.

As we have seen above, the 'psychologised' position is hardly uniform in its impact on educational discourse. Different periods have seen shifting theoretical positions within psychology. Even though the theoretical dominance of behaviourism, competency-based education, humanistic psychology and cognitive structuralism have faded, the language resources they provide are still evident in the everyday discourses of education practitioners as they debate how to style objectives, how to write educational outcomes, how to weight the importance of establishing good classroom relationships as an indicator of teaching competence, how to incorporate choice and student participation in the direction of their own learning and how to design rich learning experiences for students.

Performative Understandings

Skelton (2005) points to three features of teaching excellence in the performative approach. The first is that education, and therefore teaching, contributes directly to national economic performance through teaching that contributes to the effectiveness and competitiveness of commerce and industry. Evidence of this in contemporary times is the increasing vocationalisation of the curriculum and the stipulation of work related learner attributes as important educational outcomes (e.g. entrepreneurship, strategic thinking, flexibility, adaptability). Such an education is aimed at producing a competent and efficacious person, one who has mastered the knowledge and acquired the skills to act in the world with confidence. A person whose competence resides in continual learning, professional formation and personal development and who is critically aware of how their skills and attributes sit within the labour market – a kind of 'entrepreneur of the self'. At an institutional level this is normally measured by outcomes such as the 'employability' of graduates.

A second feature of performativity relates to the university's capacity to attract the best students in the global marketplace for higher education. The implications for teachers are that they need to be familiar with technologies which open up access to students at a distance, they need to be flexible in the way they adopt and adapt to teaching across different cultures and they need to have a global perspective on their work. The third feature is the way the state regulates teaching to ensure maximum returns on public investment. This means that data on performance needs to be gathered for public scrutiny – data related to admission standards, teaching evaluations, retention, graduations, employment outcomes and so on. The implication for teachers is that their teaching performance becomes more public and they therefore need to be mindful of the way in which they align with these measures. The purpose of this chapter is really to address how such a performative culture in teaching frames and shapes what it means to be a 'good teacher'.

Critical Understandings of Teaching

Like the psychologised approach, the critical approach contains within it a number of strands (see Brookfield, 2005). But, as Skelton (2005) points out, they all see teaching as a political activity and they are all concerned with promoting emancipation. Teaching is political in the sense that different interests are served by different curriculum and teaching practices. Casual observation of educational debate in national newspapers is clear testimony to this – for example the ongoing debates about the relative effectiveness of 'phonics' as opposed to 'whole-language' approaches to teaching is clearly driven by entrenched ideological positions, rather than by a politically neutral concern with how reading is taught. Critical theory would deny that the latter is possible and so the task of the teacher educator is to surface and critique the ideologies which support either side of the debate. Thus teaching from a critical perspective means asking questions relating to authority and control over what counts as knowledge, how knowledge is organised and transmitted, who has access to knowledge and whose interests are served by the current system.

> The teacher's main aim, from the critical perspective, is to support a process of student emancipation which seeks to give them greater control over their lives. The role of the teacher is to act as a critical or

transformative intellectual who disturbs the student's current epistemological understandings and interpretations of reality by offering new insights. . . . This involves creating teaching and learning situations which question 'common-sense' ways of thinking and behaving, leading to new forms of consciousness and ideas for effecting social and political change. (p. 33)

From a teaching perspective this involves being mindful of the way in which disciplinary cultures and curriculum and teaching practices serve to exclude certain groups of people not typical of the system as it has been forged (such as minority racial and ethnic groups, or those disadvantaged by disability or social class). This usually means adopting more participatory and inclusive teaching strategies characterised by a more democratic and collaborative teaching space. It also means adopting a critical stance as an educator, which is a key focus of this book.

The table below is a reproduction of Skelton's (2005) depiction of these four different understandings of teaching excellence in higher education.

It is worth noting that the labels Skelton uses to depict the four types are hardly neutral. For example, 'psychologised' suggested that something untoward has happened to our understanding of teaching excellence (this is certainly how Malcolm and Zukas, 2001, use the term). The very use of the term itself implies that our understanding of teaching excellence is drained of any historical, social and cultural location. While this

Table 2.1 Understandings of Teaching Excellence in Higher Education

	Traditional	Performative	Psychologised	Critical
Who for?	Social elite	Meritocracy	Individuals	Informed citizenry
Where located?	Disciplinary knowledge	Rules and regulations	Teacher–learner relationship	Material conditions
Epistemology?	Pursuit of truth	Knowledge that works	Subjective interpretation	Social critique
Indicative method?	Lecture	Work-based learning	Group work	Participatory dialogue
Teacher's role?	Subject expert	Enforcer of standards	Psycho-diagnostician	Critical intellectual
Purpose?	Cultural reproduction	System efficiency	Effective learning	Emancipation

Source: Skelton, 2005
Reproduced with permission from Taylor & Francis Books

may be true, the point can be made in the text under a more neutral label like 'psychological' rather than pre-empting the debate with a loaded term.

Skelton goes on to use these four depictions of teaching excellence as a framework for analysing how teaching excellence has been constructed and promoted through teaching award schemes in the UK (in particular the National Teaching Fellowship Scheme, which he argues is based on similar schemes in Canada, the USA and Australia). He is interested in surfacing their implicit assumptions and values as key players in the discourse of teaching excellence in higher education. The main body of his analysis is based on interviews with award winners and those responsible for setting the criteria for the scheme. He found that the following characteristics of teaching excellence were apparent:

1. Individualised – awards were made to individuals based on their individual contributions rather than team or group contributions. Therefore the idea being promoted is 'excellent teachers' rather than 'excellent teaching'.
2. An emphasis on reflective practice as a key attribute of teaching excellence together with evidence that practice developments are disseminated and shared with colleagues.
3. Psychologised reflections – where the object of reflection is the transaction between individual teachers and students (e.g. with reference to motivation, learning styles, personality).
4. Performative – a view underpinning the awards which promotes the idea that teaching excellence can be measured, controlled and improved. Also a view of education as contributing to a student's employability and career prospects.
5. Alignment with higher education policy – the award winners were either supportive of current higher education policy or prepared to work within its assumptions. Their practices and projects supported current directions (e.g. student-centred, use of new technologies, work related education, the participation agenda).

The attitude of the award winners to the scheme was interesting, as revealed by a comparison of their 'official' view of teaching excellence (as per their award application) and their 'unofficial' view as expressed in the research interviews. There were those whose official and unofficial views aligned, there were those who just 'played the game', there were those who used the scheme to support their current interests and there were those who adopted a 'strategic compliance' approach, whereby they outwardly complied while harbouring private reservations about the scheme.

Skelton (2005) summarises his findings as follows:

Through its assumptions, structures, procedures and criteria, and in the perspectives, practices and development projects undertaken by the award winners themselves, a performative and psychologised form of teaching excellence is in the making. Key aspects of a performative teaching excellence are measurement, control and system efficiency. There is an emphasis on its ability to contribute directly to national economic performance through teaching which is relevant to commerce and industry, and its commitment to instrumental progressivism which enhances the individual's opportunities for employment. A psychologised teaching excellence focuses on the transaction between individual teachers and learners, reflective practice informed by psychological theories and identifying practical solutions to teaching problems. (p. 59)

He sees in the current climate an ascendance of (and powerful alliance between) performative and psychologised understandings of teaching excellence. Powerful in the sense that they blend well with the agenda of government to increase state control over higher education and to view teaching in more instrumental terms – as if it were a craft rather than a profession, and as if 'best practice' were unproblematic, simply a matter of following the rules and prescriptions determined by evidence derived from 'scientifically robust' research. Moreover, he argues that the concepts of 'student-centred' learning and 'reflective practice' have been appropriated by both performative and psychologised discourses in a way that has drained them of their original radical intent to empower students and to promote a *critical* reflection (see p. 171).

The remainder of this chapter applies some of the above analysis to national student surveys in three countries: the US, the UK and Australia. Like teaching award schemes, national surveys serve to construct and promote views of teaching excellence. Indeed they are likely to be more potent than award schemes given that they reach to the very heart of classroom practice for the majority of teachers.

A recent review of national surveys of undergraduate students in Wales and Northern Ireland (with some Scottish institutions also participating on a voluntary basis – HEA, 2007) points to the benefits of formal student surveys:

There are arguably three main benefits to the use of formal student surveys. The first two are methodologically grounded, in that they can provide an opportunity to conduct a census of student opinions through surveying the entire student population, and that they document the experiences of the student population in a more or less systematic way, enabling year on year comparisons. These two benefits are afforded by such instruments being standardised, with associated psychometric properties of reliability and validity, which will be discussed below. The other benefit to the use of formal student surveys is that they are typically theory-based. That is, they purport to measure aspects of the student learning experience that are hypothesised to be influential on students' learning outcomes. . . . In being theory-based, formal student surveys typically contain groupings of items measuring different concepts, referred to as scales. Reliability and validity are important psychometric properties of surveys, with reliability indicating how well an instrument measures what it purports to measure, and validity indicating whether an instrument actually measures what it purports to measure. . . . Paulsen (2002) and Menges and Austin (2001) both cited in Prebble et al. (2004) suggest student ratings to be reliable and valid indicators of teaching quality.

(HEA, 2007, pp. 1–2)

We can see from the above quotation the language of performativity at work: measurement, standardisation, the need to make comparisons across the system and an unproblematised view of the relationship between educational theory and teaching quality. Also evident is a very restricted view of what constitutes 'validity'. For example the Australian survey has a number of sub-scales such as 'student support', 'appropriate assessment' and 'clear goals and standards'. Here validity is demonstrated in part by positive correlations between the sub-scales and overall student satisfaction – but this just indicates that what is being measured is student satisfaction rather than teaching quality.

We will return to this issue of validity later in the chapter, but first, we outline the three main surveys in current use in the UK, Australia and the US.

UK National Student Survey

The National Student Survey (NSS) in the UK is part of a revised Quality Assurance Framework and is delivered to final year students in all higher education institutions in England, on a voluntary basis. It was established in 2005 and is conducted annually. The questionnaire comprises 22 core questions making up 6 scales, an overall satisfaction item and then an open response item.

The items are reproduced in full in Table 2.2. Respondents are asked to indicate their agreement or disagreement on a 5 point scale with an NA column as an option. The scale options are 'Definitely agree', 'Mostly

Table 2.2 UK National Student Survey Items 2008

Scale	Items
Teaching	Staff are good at explaining things
	Staff have made the subject interesting
	Staff are enthusiastic about what they are teaching
	The course is intellectually stimulating
Assessment and feedback	The criteria used in marking have been clear in advance
	Assessment arrangements and marking have been fair
	Feedback on my work has been prompt
	I have received detailed comments on my work
	Feedback on my work has helped me clarify things I did not understand
Academic support	I have received sufficient advice and support with my studies
	I have been able to contact staff when I needed to
	Good advice was available when I needed to make study choices
Organisation and management	The timetable works efficiently as far as my activities are concerned
	Any changes in the course or teaching have been communicated effectively
	The course is well organised and is running smoothly
Learning resources	The library resources and services are good enough for my needs
	I have been able to access general IT resources when I needed to
	I have been able to access specialised equipment, facilities or rooms when I needed to
Personal development	The course has helped me to present myself with confidence
	My communication skills have improved
	As a result of the course, I feel confident in tackling unfamiliar problems
Overall satisfaction	Overall, I am satisfied with the quality of the course
Open ended questions	Highlight any positive or negative aspects of the course

Reproduced with permission from HEFCE

agree', 'Neither agree nor disagree', 'Mostly disagree' and 'Definitely disagree'.

The 2008 survey had a response rate of 60% and reveals a high overall level of satisfaction (81%). Detailed results are available on a website (Unistats, http://www.heacademy.ac.uk/hlst/news/detail/Unistats), which will allow prospective students to compare the performance of different institutions. The institutions themselves will be able to use the data to identify areas of strength and weakness, and the whole sector is supported by the newly established Higher Education Academy (HEA), which has the remit to improve the quality of teaching and learning in higher education institutions in the UK. For example, in response to the results from the NSS, the HEA commissioned research on institutions' internal student surveys with a focus on assessment and the student experience of feedback. The results of the survey are used in a variety of other ways, including universities marketing their course where they had achieved success. Its political value is also evident in the comments of the Parliamentary Under Secretary of State for Intellectual Property and Quality, Lord Triesman, who, when speaking at the launch of the 2007 NSS results, said:

> An overall satisfaction rating of 81 per cent is an excellent endorsement of higher education in this country. The NSS, and the broader information available on the new Unistats web-site, are extremely useful sources of information for potential students. The survey itself is also a helpful tool for institutions to identify areas that might need sharpening up.
>
> (HEA, 2007)

Such an endorsement positions the UK well in the global competition for students. As such there is a clear performative discourse surrounding the NSS. As far as the items are concerned, they also support Skelton's findings of a performative and psychologised discourse. This can be seen by reorganising the items under the headings of 'cognition', 'motivation', 'teacher performance', 'organisational performance' and 'personal attributes' as in Table 2.3.

There is nothing in the above items relating to the value of the content itself, the understanding of a disciplinary area or a field of practice nor any sense of a greater critical engagement with the profession or the community. Any value attached to the learning is expressed in terms of the personal attributes of the learner being enhanced, as if confidence and communication skills were all that mattered. The main emphasis is on the individual performance of the duties of the teachers and the organisational performance in fulfilling its role in supporting students.

Table 2.3 UK National Student Survey Items Organised under Different Categories 2008

Category	Items
Cognition	Staff are good at explaining things
	Feedback on my work has helped me clarify things I did not understand
Motivation	Staff have made the subject interesting
	Staff are enthusiastic about what they are teaching
	The course is intellectually stimulating
Teacher performance of duties	The criteria used in marking have been clear in advance
	Assessment arrangements and marking have been fair
	Feedback on my work has been prompt
	I have received detailed comments on my work
	I have received sufficient advice and support with my studies
	I have been able to contact staff when I needed to
	Good advice was available when I needed to make study choices
Organisational performance	The timetable works efficiently as far as my activities are concerned
	Any changes in the course or teaching have been communicated effectively
	The course is well organised and is running smoothly
	The library resources and services are good enough for my needs
	I have been able to access general IT resources when I needed to
	I have been able to access specialised equipment, facilities or rooms when I needed to
Personal attributes of learners	The course has helped me to present myself with confidence
	My communication skills have improved
	As a result of the course, I feel confident in tackling unfamiliar problems

Reproduced with permission from HEFCE

Course Experience Questionnaire Australia

Similar comments can be made about the Course Experience Questionnaire (CEQ) used in Australia, although there is less emphasis on organisational performance (see Table 2.4). In Australia all universities participate in the

Table 2.4 Course Experience Questionnaire (CEQ) Australia 2007

Items
'The staff put a lot of time into commenting on my work'
'The teaching staff normally gave me helpful feedback on how I was going'
'The course helped me develop my ability to work as a team member'
'The teaching staff of this course motivated me to do my best work'
'The course sharpened my analytic skills'
'My lecturers were extremely good at explaining things'
'The teaching staff worked hard to make their subjects interesting'
'The course developed my problem-solving skills'
'The staff made a real effort to understand difficulties I might be having with my work'
'The course improved my skills in written communication'
'As a result of my course, I feel confident about tackling unfamiliar problems'
'My course helped me to develop the ability to plan my own work'
'Overall, I was satisfied with the quality of this course'
'What were the best aspects of your course?'
'What aspects of your course were most in need of improvement?'

Source: Graduate Careers Council Australia, 2007.
Reproduced with permission from Graduate Careers Council of Australia

annual CEQ, which is undertaken by all graduating students the year immediately following the completion of their course. The items are ranked from 'Strongly disagree' to 'Strongly agree' on a 5 point scale.

The results of the CEQ are publicly available and used by universities in preparing for quality audits by the Australian Universities Quality Assurance Agency. They are also used in part to determine dividend payments to universities under the Teaching and Learning Performance Fund, a scheme administered by the federal government. Typically each university has its own internal student surveys which are heavily influenced by the CEQ.

US National Survey of Student Engagement

The approach in the US is quite different, perhaps because of the different relationship between the government in universities in the US. Exemplifying this, the development of the National Survey of Student Engagement (NSSE) was funded by a charitable organisation rather than the government. Since the pilot programme in 1999, participation in the annual NSSE has grown from 70 colleges and universities to 774 in 2008.

The survey is too broad to reproduce in its entirety but an edited version appears in Table 2.5 below, which is sufficient to illustrate the broad-ranging nature of the survey. The items not included cover the time spent in a range of activities, such as homework, field experience, study abroad, socialising, attending arts performances, and an item that covers the quality of relationships with teachers, administrative staff and other students.

Table 2.5 US National Survey of Student Engagement 2008 (Selected Items)

Selected Items

In your experience at your institution during the current school year, about how often have you done each of the following? (Very often, Often, Sometimes, Never)

Asked questions in class or contributed to class discussions

Made a class presentation

Prepared two or more drafts of a paper or assignment before turning it in

Worked on a paper or project that required integrating ideas or information from various sources

Included diverse perspectives (different races, religions, genders, political beliefs, etc.) in class discussions or writing assignments

Come to class without completing readings or assignments

Worked with other students on projects *during class*

Worked with classmates *outside of class* to prepare class assignments

Put together ideas or concepts from different courses when completing assignments or during class discussions

Tutored or taught other students (paid or voluntary)

Participated in a community-based project (e.g., service learning) as part of a regular course

Used an electronic medium (listserv, chat group, Internet, instant messaging, etc.) to discuss or complete an assignment

Used e-mail to communicate with an instructor

Discussed grades or assignments with an instructor

Talked about career plans with a faculty member or advisor

Discussed ideas from your readings or classes with faculty members outside of class

Received prompt written or oral feedback from faculty on your academic performance

Worked harder than you thought you could to meet an instructor's standards or expectations

(*Continued overleaf*)

Table 2.5 Continued

Selected Items

Worked with faculty members on activities other than coursework (committees, orientation, student life activities, etc.)

Discussed ideas from your readings or classes with others outside of class (students, family members, co-workers, etc.)

Had serious conversations with students of a different race or ethnicity than your own

Had serious conversations with students who are very different from you in terms of their religious beliefs, political opinions, or personal values

During the current school year, how much has your coursework emphasized the following mental activities? (Very much, Quite a bit, Some, Very little)

Memorizing facts, ideas, or methods from your courses and readings so you can repeat them in pretty much the same form

Analyzing the basic elements of an idea, experience, or theory, such as examining a particular case or situation in depth and considering its components

Synthesizing and organizing ideas, information, or experiences into new, more complex interpretations and relationships

Making judgments about the value of information, arguments, or methods, such as examining how others gathered and interpreted data and assessing the soundness of their conclusions

Applying theories or concepts to practical problems or in new situations

To what extent does your institution emphasize each of the following?

(Very much, Quite a bit, Some, Very little)

Spending significant amounts of time studying and on academic work

Providing the support you need to help you succeed academically

Encouraging contact among students from different economic, social, and racial or ethnic backgrounds

Helping you cope with your non-academic responsibilities (work, family, etc.)

Providing the support you need to thrive socially

Attending campus events and activities (special speakers, cultural performances, athletic events, etc.)

Using computers in academic work

To what extent has your experience at this institution contributed to your knowledge, skills, and personal development in the following areas?

(Very much, Quite a bit, Some, Very little)

Acquiring a broad general education

Acquiring job or work-related knowledge and skills

Writing clearly and effectively

Speaking clearly and effectively

Thinking critically and analytically

Analyzing quantitative problems

Using computing and information technology

Working effectively with others

Voting in local, state, or national elections

Learning effectively on your own

Understanding yourself

Understanding people of other racial and ethnic backgrounds

Solving complex real-world problems

Developing a personal code of values and ethics

Contributing to the welfare of your community

Developing a deepened sense of spirituality

Reproduced with permission from The College Student Report, *National survey of student engagement*, Copyright 2001–08 The Trustees of Indiana University

The focus of the items is on the educational experiences of the students and how they spend their time. The items are derived from empirical work linking high-quality student outcomes with particular kinds of classroom, peer and staff activities and practices. In effect, the characteristics of the student experience are used as a proxy for quality. The results are used by institutions to improve aspects of student engagement known to improve such outcomes. They have also been used for benchmarking purposes, in the dissemination of good practice, and they are increasingly being used for accreditation with the focus shifting away from resources and inputs and towards outcomes. The broad ranging nature of the survey means that the information generated can be used, not only by institutions and prospective students, but by other stakeholders such as counsellors, academic advisers and researchers to better understand how students spend their time. The items have a focus on diversity; the full range of experiences in learning and living while a student; generic cognitive skills such as memorising, synthesising, and thinking critically; and generic personal skills including political and community engagement.

As such this is more than a survey of student satisfaction, in fact there are relatively few evaluative questions. It really documents the kinds of experiences that students are exposed to while they are a student at a particular institution. While many of the questions are value laden (e.g. a developing sense of spirituality) and open to debate, and while many fall into the 'psychologised' category, overall the survey is not imbued with a performative discourse. There is very little emphasis on the skills and qualities of individual teachers, or even organisational performance, but rather the emphasis is on how the system as a whole shapes the experiences of students. The items as a whole assume that a university is responsible in some way for the total development of the students – for example, by supporting them to develop social networks, engage in the political process and contribute to community life. Overall the NSSE does not seem to foreclose debate about what constitutes quality teaching, instead the very scope of its questions allows space to engage in the kinds of contestation about quality teaching that are important for a healthy higher education system.

Concluding Comments

This chapter has looked at the issue of quality teaching from the point of view of the instruments in place designed to reward or measure quality teaching. The various awards for teaching that exist in the UK, Australia and the US contain within them explicit (and sometimes implicit) views of what constitutes good teaching. Likewise the various national surveys of students contain within them assumptions about what constitutes good teaching. Such surveys, moreover, typically frame institutional approaches to measuring quality, and ultimately the way in which individual teachers develop their teaching evaluation portfolios, for the purposes of securing an academic position, a promotion, a tenure or simply as part of annual performance reviews. This whole system we referred to as a performative culture, in the sense that performance at the system, institutional and individual level is monitored and measured. We are not arguing that this is a wholly bad thing, but that we should recognise the limitations of the system and adopt a critical approach to any instrument that serves to cut off debate about what it means to be a good teacher. Additionally we need to consider our approach to how we align ourselves with these instruments. Do we take them seriously as measures of quality teaching and align our views accordingly? Do we adopt a pragmatic approach and comply with all requirements while taking a different personal view? Do we just use them strategically to advance our careers? What are the personal and professional costs of adopting one or another of these strategies? For example, can we sustain a conflict between our public position and our personal position? In complying with externally imposed measures are we eventually shaped by our actions so that these measures and our own position become indistinguishable? Whatever position is taken, we argue that it is important to understand the way in which teaching evaluations shape and frame the discourse of 'good teaching' and that we should recognise such discourse when we encounter it in everyday working life.

Enhancing Professional Practice

Step 1. List the information/feedback you would like to gather from students in order to improve your teaching. List these as potential items for an evaluation to be conducted with your students. Note that the focus here is on improving your teaching rather than proving the value of your teaching to others.

Step 2. Locate a survey instrument that is used by a university (your own or another) to gather information about teaching quality.

Step 3. Compare the items in the survey instrument to those that you have developed. How do they differ? How do your items reveal a view of good teaching that is different from that contained in the survey instrument?

Step 4. Discuss your ideas from Step 3 with a colleague.

CHAPTER 3

Reconceptualising the Development of University Teaching Expertise

Introduction

Chapter 2 explored different understandings of quality teaching in higher education and analysed the way in which national teaching award schemes and national and institutional student evaluation surveys largely promoted a performative understanding. We argued that such schemes provide a framework and a discourse that partly shapes our evolving understanding of what it means to be a good teacher. As such the chapter sought to deconstruct the assumptions underlying prevailing frameworks, which arguably allows us to pose the question anew: What is good quality teaching and how can academics develop and sustain the capacity to be good or excellent teachers?

The purpose of this chapter is to engage with both parts of this question. In doing so, teaching will be considered a work practice, and so the issues and perspectives present in Chapter 8 on workplace-oriented learning are also pertinent here. The argument in this chapter is that in times of change, dominant understandings of expertise do not align well with contemporary academic workplaces characterised by complexity and uncertainty. Traditional understandings of expertise tend to focus on the individual and regard expertise as stable and enduring and knowledge based. However, teaching expertise can be conceptualised quite differently, and more appropriately, by giving greater emphasis to the sociocultural factors and by viewing teacher identity as something that is dynamic, multiple and provisional rather than fixed and unitary.

We argue that drawing together the concepts of expertise and identity provides the opportunity for an innovative way to theorise and better understand the development of university teaching expertise. This socially situated view of expertise acknowledges both the dynamic and relational nature of expertise and the social and cultural positioning of university teachers. At several points in the chapter we will introduce teacher 'voices' drawn from a recent narrative study of the development of teaching expertise undertaken by one of the authors (McMullen, 2008).

Teaching Expertise

A good starting point for understanding what constitutes good teaching is to consider the skills, knowledge and attributes of those who are regarded as 'expert teachers'. There exists a tradition of research which has sought to analyse the nature of expertise across a range of different occupations and activities such as chess playing. This research has been largely influenced by cognitive psychology and has been applied to teaching. Berliner (1987; 1994; 2001; 2004), in particular, draws on the general expertise literature to describe and document the behaviour and accomplishments of expert teachers. Whilst acknowledging that the link between expert teachers and their students' performance is not as easy to establish as the link between expert chess and bridge players and their performance, Berliner (1994) argues that many of the propositions about expertise in general (Chi, Glaser & Farr, 1988) can equally be used to describe teachers. Specifically Berliner claims that:

- Experts excel mainly in their own domain and in particular contexts.
- Experts often develop automaticity for the repetitive operations that are needed to accomplish their goals.
- Experts are more sensitive to the task demands and social situation when solving problems.
- Experts are more opportunistic and flexible in their teaching than novices.
- Experts represent problems in qualitatively different ways than do novices.
- Experts have fast and accurate pattern recognition capabilities.
- Experts perceive meaningful patterns in the domain in which they are experienced.
- Experts may begin to solve problems slower but they bring richer and more personal sources of information to bear on the problems that they are trying to solve.

(Berliner, 1994, pp. 167–179)

Consistent with the general arguments about expertise Berliner (1994) claims that time and experience play a significant role in the development of pedagogical expertise. While experience alone will not make a teacher an expert, Berliner suggests that it is likely that almost every expert teacher has had extensive classroom experience. We know that experience is important, but how is experience utilised to gain expertise and what is the role of the teacher or trainer? In this regard it is crucial to distinguish between expertise as an outcome and the acquisition of expertise as a process. For example, in Chi et al.'s (1988) summary of the generic qualities of expertise they note that experts are faster and more economical, partly because they do not conduct an extensive search of the data or information available. This does not imply that novices should be warned against conducting extensive searches of the data or urged to take short cuts. Quite the contrary, extensive searches of the data (using standard abstract algorithms – perhaps learnt 'out of context') are presumably important at the novice stage, and in this sense expertise is built upon the experience of being a novice. But it may be that the generic qualities of expertise are actually developed from experience and not from the application of 'fundamental' principles to experience. Alignment on this issue demarcates different approaches to professional development. For example, in the case of academic staff development, an approach which sought to impart 'fundamental principles' would typically be organised centrally within the university, and comprise a curriculum which covered a range of educational theories and practices which were largely decontextualised. It would then be the responsibility of the learners to apply these theories and practices to their own context. An approach which viewed generic skills as only being developed through experience would comprise an experience-based curriculum which largely covered the skills which enhanced the learners' capacity to learn from experience. But is there such a thing: a generic skill relating to learning from experience? The answer to this question too would affect how educators approach academic staff development.

The literature on expertise seems to answer in the affirmative – that there are generic skills of this kind.

It is clear from a reading of the literature that expertise is built on a number of generic capacities that can be utilised in different contexts: such as problem formation, self-monitoring skills, higher-order principled thinking and flexibility and adaptability to the environment in problem solving. While domain specific expertise is acknowledged, generic expertise seems to be more highly valued. Symptomatic of this is Prerau, Adler and Gunderson's (1992) labelling of experience-based knowledge as 'shallow' and knowledge of the fundamental principles of a domain as 'deep'. Why are these metaphors applied in this way? We suggest it is because the fundamental project of the strand of cognitive psychology, which informs much of the expertise literature, is to identify generic models of cognitive functioning, and this depends crucially on some level of expertise which is fundamental and cuts across different contexts. Thus, while cognitive psychology attempts to come to terms with the 'problem' of context, its traditional focus on the individual as the site of cognitive activity and the repository of knowledge precludes it from adequately addressing the 'social' dimensions of expertise. Much of the literature on teacher expertise, influenced strongly by educational psychology, has taken a knowledge-based view of teaching with a focus on the individual teacher. 'Good teaching' is seen as being developed primarily through cognitive structuring of learning experiences in ways that facilitate reflection on theory in relation to experience (Nicoll & Harrison, 2003). Little attention, however, is given to understanding learning as social practice or to considering the changing contexts of university teaching.

This is precisely what Kemmis (2005) warns against:

> privileging knowledge 'in people's heads' over the social and discursive orders that support that knowledge. To avoid this danger, practitioners wanting to understand the world of practice must also enter the discursive and social realms of practice at a meta-level, consciously seeing themselves as shaped by modes of practice and ideas about practice that are part of a shared social and discursive world with its own distinctive modes of structuration that exist 'outside' the heads of individual practitioners (even if they can only be apprehended cognitively, that is, by knowing subjects). (p. 402)

For this reason we argue that focusing on an expert teacher's knowledge structure and level of experience presents a static view of expertise that does not align well with a changing academic environment. It does not tell us how expert teachers developed their expertise or how they maintain their expertise in times of change. It also fails to explain why people reach different levels of expertise. Underlying assumptions in this expertise literature are an autonomous self, a relatively stable environment and an enduring knowledge base that can be applied in a range of contexts. This static view of expertise is not well suited to workplaces characterised by change, complexity and diversity.

As Light and Cox (2001) argue, the 'excellence' debates have often failed to address the substance and complexity of the challenges in teaching and learning.

'Excellence' has often elicited approaches for developing expertise in teaching and learning which address the new state of complexity by imposing a 'reductionist' (and 'accounting') framework to simplify it. Curiously, they engage the uncertain by assuming, as Barnett notes 'a known situation and well understood attributes' (1997a: 41). The result is an approach that specifies increasingly narrow outcomes and competencies of expertise, establishes behavioural standards for them and insists on compliance with these standards irrespective of the professional, disciplinary and institutional context (ILT 1999a). (p. 10)

An essential part of teaching expertise must be the capacity to transform and change the very conception of 'expertise' in response to altered teaching conditions. Thus expertise, like learning, needs to be conceptualised as process rather than a point of attainment (see Hager, 2004, cited in Chapter 8).

This is exemplified in the approach of Bereiter and Scardamalia (1993). Borrowing from the field of psychometric intelligence, they make a distinction between fluid and crystallised expertise in an attempt to better understand the development of expertise. Crystallised expertise refers to the form of expertise consisting of intact procedures, well learned through previous experience. Fluid expertise, by contrast, consists of abilities brought into play on novel or challenging tasks or tasks that the expert has elected to treat in a challenging way. They suggest that these two forms of expertise interact in a dynamic process with fluid expertise being converted into crystallised expertise and crystallised expertise providing a basis for the future growth of fluid expertise. This thinking underlies their description of expertise as a process. They argue that in domains where expertise flourishes problems tend not to have ceilings on them. That is, there is always a higher level at which the problem can be approached. Thus problem solving becomes progressive.

From this perspective, expertise must consist of something that goes over and above the normal course of learning with experts continually pushing themselves to higher levels of performance through ongoing self-regulation. Self-regulatory knowledge, according to Bereiter and Scardamalia (1993), is self-knowledge relevant to performance in a domain and can be thought of as knowledge that controls the application of other knowledge. Expertise is thus dynamic (rather than a point of attainment) characterised by continuous efforts to surpass one's earlier achievement and work at the edge of one's competence.

While extending the concept of expertise to include continuous self-improvement during a career is a useful development this only addresses part of the dynamic nature of expertise. Teaching expertise is not only brought to the classroom, it is put into practice in the classroom and involves interaction with students. The quest for constant improvement may help foster the development of teaching expertise, but development as a teacher involves much more than technique. Teaching is a social activity as Olson (1992) observes:

> Teaching takes place in a communal world with shared meaning. This world is held together by commitments to certain values which neophytes (or novices) have to learn. It is through belonging to the world of teaching that teachers are able to do what they do. (p. 22)

Viewing teaching expertise from a perspective of practice rather than knowledge moves the focus from the individual and locates the learning and expertise of an individual teacher within the wider social and cultural context of university teaching. Professional development becomes not just a matter of teachers developing enhanced cognitive capacities but also a question of coming to know their culture in more productive ways (Olson, 1992). Alternative positions on expertise are thus needed that reflect the complexity of expertise and promote an understanding of the process of the development of expertise.

Teacher Excellence as Identity Work

With the 'enterprise' university presenting new and varied demands on university teachers, conceptions of teaching expertise and teacher identity as stable and enduring are no longer sustainable. In these times of complexity and uncertainty in universities when academic identities are being challenged, competing views emerge about what it means to be an expert teacher. Thus we need a contextualised view of teaching expertise that acknowledges both the dynamic and relational nature of expertise and the social and cultural positioning of university teachers. As such, developing teaching expertise is not simply a matter of acquiring new skills and knowledge – it is about taking up new identities, new ways of understanding and conducting oneself.

In using identity as a frame within which to examine teaching expertise we are not presenting a view of 'teacher self' as coherent, unified and fixed, a perspective that has underpinned much of the academic development literature. Rather, we draw on the work of Giddens (1991), Rose (1996), Hall (1996), du Gay (1997), Edwards (1997), Bruner and Kalmar (1998) and Chappell, Rhodes, Solomon, Tennant and Yates (2003), that share an understanding of identity as multiple, positional and strategic; always under construction. This narrative view of identity brings to the fore the social situation of the self. The narrative structures that we use to organise our life are not of our own making – they are socially embedded and culturally transmitted. Thus the ability for a person to narrate their own life (professional as well as personal) is both limited and enabled by the narrative resources they are able to draw on. In this way, the self remains situated in history and culture and continually open to reinscription, as Hall (1996) explains:

> identities are about questions of using the resources of history, language and culture in the process of becoming rather than being: not 'who we are' or 'where we came from' so much as who we might become, how we have been represented and how that bears on how we might represent ourselves. (p. 4)

Developing reflexivity thus plays a central role in this process of developing teaching expertise. University teachers need to go beyond simply adapting to change – they need to engage with change and understand how they see themselves as a teacher and how others attempt to position them. This capacity for reflexivity – self and social questioning – is part of negotiating a trajectory through the insecurities and risks associated with change (Edwards, Ranson & Strain, 2002). Given the rapid changes in the workplace, attaining a specific body of knowledge is less important than the ability to learn. Expertise can be viewed as a lifelong learning project where identity is fashioned and refashioned over time.

This marked shift away from a static view of expertise arguably suits contemporary times. Contemporary individuals, experiencing a much wider range of life options and possibilities than previous generations, are increasingly being expected to take greater control of their life choices than was the case in the past. The dynamic process through which individuals make meaning of their lives and incorporate these meaning into future action forms the basis of Giddens' concept of 'the reflexive project of the self'. Giddens (1991) describes self-identity as a reflexively organised endeavour where:

> The reflexive project of the self, which consists in the sustaining of coherent, yet continuously revised, biographical narratives, takes place in a context of multiple choice. . . . Each of us not only "has," but lives a biography reflexively organized in terms of social and psychological information about possible ways of life. (pp. 5, 14)

The self is not a passive entity, determined by external influences. The subject as understood by Giddens is highly self-conscious, constantly engaged in identity work and seeking narrative coherence, if only on a transitory basis. Reflexivity also plays an important role in connecting personal and social change (Giddens, 1991) and surfacing possible choices. Identity, viewed in this way, is not an object to be examined but a reality constructed in the interactive moment (McNamee, 1996). Thus, it is always a work in progress, an individual enterprise played out through social interaction. Identity is not something that the individual 'is' but something that emerges through relations (Jensen & Westenholz, 2004).

Narrative discourses display 'the imprint of the culture and its institutions on the individual's sense of identity' (Eakin, 1999, p. 33). An example from teaching can be found in Malcolm and Zukas' (2001) analysis of the *psychologisation of teaching and learning,* which they claim is a dominant framework for shaping a particular way of 'knowing' about teachers, learners and educational practices in higher education. University teachers, however, can and will resist, in varying degrees, dominant discourses. (A detailed discussion around the psychologisation of teaching and learning can be found in Chapter 2.)

Clearly teachers draw on their own learning experiences to shape their views on 'good teaching'. The excerpts from interviews presented in Table 3.1 illustrate the way personal biography shapes views on what constitutes 'good teaching' with university teachers bringing much more than knowledge and skills to the classroom. As Wenger (1998, p. 145) suggests, 'There is a profound connection between identity and practice. Practice enables the negotiation of being a person in that context.' The left-hand side of Table 3.1 contains specific quotes about positive learning experiences that have influenced these teachers' constructions of good teaching. Moving to the right-hand side of the table, parallels between teachers' own experiences and what they consider to be 'good teaching' can be clearly recognised.

For Joy, creativity and performance are an essential part of 'good teaching'. She sees them as fundamental for engaging students and keeping them 'on task'. Like Miss White who produced 'a new thing every day' Joy likes to bring 'novelty' to what she does and reciprocate 'the freshness that students bring to her'. Teaching as performance is a constant theme in Joy's narrative. For her 'good teaching' requires 'a flair for entertaining' and metaphors reinforcing this view of teaching as performance are common in her story. From her earliest experiences of what teachers did she 'was aware of the preparation side and how the rehearsal of teaching happens.'

David identifies his high school experience as critical in shaping his views about the importance of peer learning. His story highlights the importance he sees of being engaged, learning as part of a community and following the areas for which you have a passion. All this is more important than just getting good grades. This is echoed in his views on good teaching that stress the ongoing nature of learning, the collaborative nature of learning and learning as a way of bringing about social change.

Carolyn nominates her father as a critical influence on the way she thinks about teaching. Discussion about teaching and learning were an everyday part of her home life and she grew up with the idea of education as exciting and as an arena where everything is open to question. Her view of teaching as dynamic and involving 'continual questioning' mirrors the views on education that she was exposed to through her father.

Table 3.1 Positive Learning Experiences Shaping Views on 'Good Teaching'

Positive learning experiences	Views on 'good teaching'
What stands out – two teachers I think, Miss White was about 80, I'm pretty sure, when I was about 3 years old and I used to race out and meet her at the bus in the morning. So I was too young to go [to school] but what I used to do was watch her draw on the blackboard and practise the music and generally have that feeling that she took time to prepare and that the class was coming and she had all of those things ready. (Joy)	I think the thing is to bring novelty you know to actually know that even though some things have been around for a long time, you meet the students with the kind of freshness that they bring to you . . . So over the years I might have taught similar things but every year the students are different. They come from a slightly different culture, a slightly different way of seeing things. (Joy)
So I was aware of the preparation side and how the rehearsal of teaching happens, and also thought that it was such a gift that somebody would do all that drawing on the blackboard. . . . Yes, and there would be a new thing every day. So it was not something that was staid and I guess that also impressed me that every day she came and did something that hadn't been done before. It was very, very creative. (Joy)	Good teaching is a flair for entertaining, for learning. That's really, really important! So that students will engage and be on task. I like catching them out . . . when I used to take on the game show type things or the Oprah Winfrey or Jerry Springer or whatever else I would come up with. The thing was that the students didn't even realise that in there was all of the stuff that they were going to have to take away. (Joy)
I went to an alternative high school and we were encouraged to do some teaching so I taught some of my peers at high school. . . . I went from being a very withdrawn student who said nothing but did reasonably well in the existing system to someone who didn't do quite as well in terms of my final mark. But I was much more engaged in my learning and taught courses in things I loved. So that's perhaps one reason I had the confidence and interest to become a teacher later on. (David)	Good teaching is intuitive. It's based on constant learning . . . It's based on peer learning because we all teach each other. It's about thinking outside your box . . . It's about social change. (David)

(*Continued overleaf*)

Table 3.1 Continued

Positive learning experiences	Views on 'good teaching'
My father was a highly innovative educator . . . and he published in that area and conversation around the meal table from almost when I can remember, I think I was about four . . . Why do you have to set exams? What experiential learning can students do? So that was all in me that education is exciting, interesting. You've got to think about how it works. You're allowed to question everything rather than just say well that's how it's always been done. (Carolyn)	[Good teaching] I think is the continual questioning, continual reflecting, continual seeking for balance . . . One of the core things of my tutorials is that there is never an answer, there's only another question and I always say to the students, 'If you come out of my tutorials with more questions than answers I have succeeded. Don't feel uncomfortable at the end of the tutorial if you know more about what you don't know than about what you do know. At least you've started thinking'. And you talk about golden moments, you know, one of the nicest things was in one of those feedback things where somebody wrote, 'I think this subject should be renamed "Thinking 101" '. (Carolyn)

Negative learning experiences can also have a powerful impact on understandings of 'good teaching'. This will be illustrated in Chapter 4 which explores teacher–learner relationships.

Following du Gay (1997) this shaping of practice through experience can be conceptualised as teachers assembling and deploying their personal experience and identities as learners in delivering 'good teaching'. Du Gay (1997) argues (in relation to service workers) that people are not born with the capacity or disposition to provide 'quality service'. Rather they are worked on or in turn work on themselves to become the sort of people who would offer 'quality service'. The idea of being 'made up' suggests a process of formation or transformation, that is a 'fashioning' whereby the adoption of certain habits or dispositions allows an individual to become – and become recognised as – a particular kind of person. To be made up as a worker is therefore to acquire a particular assemblage of attributes and dispositions that defines a particular set of work activities at any given period or in any given context.

If identity is viewed as constructed and reflexive rather than a fixed entity, what implications does this have for how we understand university teacher identities? Three key issues can be identified in addressing this question.

First, there is no fixed single 'teacher identity'. Because there are numerous available discourses, a number of subject positions are produced.

Given the multiplicity of competing and contradictory discourses, subjectivity is regarded as multiple, with individuals and groups having access to a repertoire of socially available positions.

There is no ideal university teacher to which new teachers must conform. As Malcolm and Zukas (2001) suggest:

> 'becoming an educator' is actually a process of realising that there is no fixed, external 'pedagogic identity' into which novice teachers must try to fit themselves. . . . Pedagogic identity is not a secret formula to be learned, or a ready-made garment in which we can clothe ourselves. It is the product of a process of identity construction, undertaken in the contexts of 'knowledge-work' and overlapping forms of community membership. (n.p.)

Relating this perspective to the development of teaching expertise lends support to the argument that there are multiple expressions of university teaching expertise and multiple paths in developing teaching expertise.

Second, we need to understand teacher identity not in the abstract but always in relation to a given place and time. As Sarup (1996) suggests:

> Our identity is not separate from what has happened . . . When asked about identity, we start thinking about our life-story: we construct our identity at the same time as we tell our life-story. (p. 15)

Representation of identity is an ongoing process and an important aspect in the construction and negotiation of identity is the past–present relationship (Sarup, 1996). The past will be interpreted and reinterpreted in the light of the present. Subject formation is a never-ending story, played out compulsively again and again. However, these identities are not created from thin air, they are available to use through culturally available narratives. Identity work aligns to pre-existing and socioculturally shaped subject positions to reproduce dominant beliefs, interests and values (Ivanic, 1998, cited in Chappell et al., 2003).

Third, teacher identity is not merely a personal choice – it is subject to affirmation by others. The development of teaching expertise involves becoming an authorised and an authoritative teacher within a scholarly community. John, an award winning teacher participating in the narrative study discussed earlier in this chapter (McMullen, 2008), observes:

> The point at which you start to appreciate that you know more than you think you do is when people start coming to you for advice or students leave the room and say, 'Gee that was good John' or 'Thanks John' or whatever. And it's just those little things, you know, that you

feed on and you puff your chest out and think, I can do a bit better next time. Or I can take a bit more of a leap next time. . . . I thought I was actually contributing something back to the academic group in terms of the case studies I was developing, I was giving them contacts to industry, I've brought in industry people. And that's what happens to me. The chest comes out, I start walking taller, straighter, and all of a sudden this humble working class boy gets to strut his stuff. I get a buzz from that.

University teachers come to understand themselves as subjects within a public community.

The term 'social acceptance' is used by Shotter (1989) to describe the fact that we must talk in particular established ways – that is, account for ourselves – in order to meet the demands placed on us by our need to sustain our status as responsible members of society. Where certain ways of talking are considered legitimate and others not, our understanding and experience of ourselves will be similarly constrained.

These three key issues are aptly brought together by Holmes (1999) describing the fashioning of identity as:

the continuing process by which a person seeks to attain and maintain uniqueness and individuality (personal being) while also being socially recognised (social being). This involves the 'appropriation' by the individual of the characteristics of socially and culturally (and therefore discursively) legitimated identities. From this follows a stage of 'transformation', making personal sense of the socially acquired understanding, in terms of personal experiences. The 'publication' of the actor's claim to the identity, the public expression of the characteristics associated with the identity leads, if successful, to 'conventionalisation' into the personal biography and social order. (p. 93)

The process of identity formation involves a dynamic relationship between the individual's sense of self and the social processes that to a significant degree determine what count as the criteria for being ascribed a particular identity. Thus, an identity cannot be decided solely by an individual, as a personal act of choice and will, but must always be subject to affirmation.

Table 3.2 summarises the key differences between what we portray as the 'traditional perspective' on the development of teaching expertise, and our view of how it should be reconceptualised.

The key differences in Table 3.2 are a connection between the personal and the social in contrast to a focus on the individual; a dynamic, fluid and contested view of expertise rather than a static and enduring one; and a view

Table 3.2 Differing Perspectives on the Development of Teaching Expertise

Traditional perspective	Reconceptualisation
Expertise as relatively *enduring*	Expertise as *dynamic, fluid, contested*
Expertise acquired through *deliberate practice* over extended periods	Expertise developed and sustained though *reflexive practice*
Stable environment allows cumulative learning (around 10 years to develop expertise)	*Ongoing change* necessitating flexibility and learning across lifespan
Structured learning – involving effortful adaptation	Diversity in learning practices – *informal learning* important
Individual activity	Activity embedded in *social structures* and *cultural contexts* of interpretation
Focus on *what* is learnt	Focus on *how* learning takes place
Professional growth	*Professional and personal* growth
Autonomous self	Identity *fashioned* and refashioned
Personal change	*Personal and social* change connected though reflexive process

of the self as multiple, positional and strategic, always under construction; rather than a view of self that is autonomous, coherent, and fixed.

This reconceptualisation of teaching expertise throws up a range of challenges to existing professional development programmes for university teachers. First, there is the challenge of developing genuinely reflexive practitioners, which, in part, means practitioners who can engage with and critique the competing discourses on what it means to be a good teacher. Second, accepting that the development of teaching expertise is largely through the experience of teaching, teaching sites need to be given greater acknowledgement as sites of professional development and thus receive institutional support for localised professional development. The implications of these challenges will be discussed in the following section.

Rethinking Professional Development for University Teachers

In times of ongoing change and challenges in their workplace, academic development is an important resource for university teachers. But, given the complex, dynamic and situated nature of teaching expertise, how should such development be configured and what should be the balance between formal and informal learning? The argument so far suggests that greater acknowledgement needs to be given to the local and ongoing nature of professional development and to the role of informal learning. Boud (1999) agrees, claiming that most academic development takes place in locations where academics spend the majority of their time and that the practice of academic development needs to be grounded in the nature of academic work. As Andresen (2000) observes: 'vast numbers of teachers manage to acquire and/or develop this knowledge [teacher knowledge] at a very substantial level of expertise, without formal instruction or training whatever' (p. 146).

Despite the arguments put to date, a case can be made that formal programmes still have an important role to play in a number of key areas: (1) induction of new staff; (2) introducing teachers to a range of theoretical frames that provide ideas and language to explore their teaching experiences; (3) where new systems are instituted on a university wide basis, for example, a new online learning system; (4) in areas where disciplinary diversity is productive for planned outcomes; and (5) where programmes are needed that challenge the taken-for-grantedness of local ways of operating.

Notwithstanding the above, the development of teaching expertise is best conceptualised as a lifelong learning project, the 'learning' in that lifelong project comprises more than simply focusing on acquisition of 'teacher knowledge'. Consideration needs to be given to learning as social practice situated in particular communities as well as to the provisional nature of knowledge.

> Learning . . . is not a process of individual knowledge construction within a socially and culturally stable situation, but is fragmented, uncertain and changing precisely because it is constructed in this increasingly fragmented, uncertain and changing world.
>
> (Light & Cox, 2001, p. 45)

This uncertainty highlights the need for reflexivity in the development of teaching expertise. Both self-monitoring and monitoring of relationships with others are ongoing activities in the development of teaching expertise and the fashioning of teacher identity. To support the development of teaching expertise consideration needs to be given to creating spaces, both private and public, for this reflexive practice.

Before proceeding to discuss in detail potential initiatives at the local level to support the development of teaching expertise, it is important to outline four key principles that we argue should underpin these activities: (1) an acknowledgement of learning as central to sustaining and reshaping expertise in times of change; (2) a view of learning that recognises uncertainty and complexity; (3) a recognition of and respect for diversity in the development and expression of expertise; and (4) the need for all university teachers to develop an informed personal perspective on 'teaching excellence' and what it means for their practice (Skelton, 2005).

Suggesting ways to support the development of teaching expertise is by no means a straightforward undertaking. Commenting on establishing 'productive reflection' in workplaces, Docherty, Boud and Cressey (2006) highlight the need to attain a balance between the formal design of conditions for productive reflection and the provision of flexibility for the development of informal practices. Three areas of activity, however, provide scope to support the development of teaching expertise in sites of teaching practice. These are: (1) writing about teaching; (2) developing learning communities around teaching; and (3) developing 'deliberate relationships' with students.

Writing about Teaching: Private and Public

Many authors attest to the power of writing in coming to know and understand oneself and others. Given the argued importance of reflexivity in the development of teaching expertise, writing, both public and private, warrants greater attention for the role it can play in professional development. Richardson (2001), for example, comments that:

> Writing was the method through which I constituted the world and reconstituted myself. Writing became my principal tool through which I learned about myself and the world. I wrote so I would have a life. Writing was and is how I come to know. (p. 33)

McMullen's research (2008) on personal narratives of the development of teachers' expertise found that the ongoing refashioning of expertise, a lifelong learning project, was always in play. John's story below illustrates this:

> Because I was willing to change and I had a tendency to get bored and I wanted to put those challenges out, I just did it. I just did them. I didn't have a view that this is what the end game was. But in hindsight, if I could paint a picture of what it all looks like . . . trying to understand what is it that drives you. And just reflecting back on all these things, I realise that it actually makes sense . . . .
>
> That all formed the basis for how I progressed into an academic teacher. What did I learn from that? I learned that you have to inspire. To motivate people you have to, I guess, lead by example in some sense. And I think that is still me. Trying to show people the way by doing and encouraging. I think it is also about being genuinely inquisitive and realising when you are in a situation where you are teaching you are also learning. They're a duality.
>
> (John)

This passage highlights the need for teachers to have the capacity to restory in times of change, to produce new and different understandings of self and other. Private writing about teaching is one way to provide a space for challenging existing understandings and develop new perspectives. Van Manen (1997), in his book *Researching lived experience*, speaks to the power of writing in developing self-awareness:

> Writing teaches us what we know, and in what way we know we know what we know. As we commit ourselves to paper we see ourselves mirrored in this text. Now this text confronts us . . . Writing creates a distance between ourselves and the world whereby the subjectivities of daily experience become the object of our reflective awareness. (p. 127)

Journals and teaching portfolios provide private reflective writing spaces. However, there is also opportunity for a greater sharing of experience through public writing, for instance in a writing group. This would provide a structure to develop public writing to further the scholarship of teaching. Central to the idea of scholarship of teaching is 'an artifact, a product, some form of community property that can be shared, discussed, critiqued, exchanged, built upon' (Shulman, 1993, p. 7). Texts produced in writing groups could provide a basis for discussion within local groups and open much broader conversations about particular aspects of teaching and learning through the production of conference papers and journal articles.

The value of writing groups has been discussed in regard to research writing at the departmental level to address demands for increased research productivity (Lee & Boud, 2003) and within research degrees (Aitchison & Lee, 2006). However, little attention has been given to writing groups focused around teaching and learning as a way to support the development of teaching expertise and build scholarship of teaching. The arguments that Lee and Boud (2003) advance, in regard to research development as local practice, can equally be applied to teaching practice. They argue that questions of change pose threats and opportunities to individuals, often challenging the fundamental conception of self and self-worth, and attention needs to be given to the emotional dimensions of development and change. They advocate bringing academics into productive relationships with each other, to identify and support fundamental values and activities. They present writing groups, a practice that exemplifies peer learning in the workplace, as one way to address the need for a contextualised local approach to academic development.

The development of teaching expertise has been conceptualised in this chapter as identity work. There is a tendency to think of academic identity in terms of a local context, but Lee and Boud (2003) observe (in regard to research) that for academics in an era of rapidly accelerating globalisation of higher education, the peer-reviewed journal becomes a key site where identity is performed and recognised. With increased emphasis on scholarship of teaching and teaching as community property, a similar case can be made for teacher identity work taking place on a wider stage.

Developing Learning Communities around Teaching

In this book we have drawn attention to the situated nature of workplace learning and discussed learning as social practice. While teaching is often thought of as an individual activity, increasingly there are demands for university teachers to be more accountable and to accept more public scrutiny of their teaching practice. In addition, opening up new spaces and new connections in teaching practice is often more productive and pleasurable in the company of others. Existing and new perspectives can be tested and extended as MacIntyre (1987) observes:

> one can only think for oneself if one does not think by oneself. . . . It is only through the discipline of having one's ideas tested in ongoing debate . . . that the reasoning of any particular individual is rescued from the vagaries of passion and interest. (p. 24)

The development of learning communities, gatherings of teachers with similar interests, can foster a collaborative and reflective culture around teaching practice. Writing groups, discussed above, are one example of a learning community. Learning communities could be large or small, formal or informal, centred around interests such as assessment design, online learning or preparation of students for professional practice. Advances in technology have created a wide range of possibilities for virtual learning communities including communities connected on a global basis. We can now start to imagine and implement professional development in diverse yet connected communities across disciplinary and national boundaries. One example of this would be an online connected community developing and sharing digital resources and engaging in robust and wide-reaching discussions about the raft of pedagogical affordances created through 'Web 2.0' services such as blogs and wikis and sites such as 'YouTube'. Through participation in learning communities we can broaden our horizons in terms of teaching practice, communication and knowledge creation.

'Deliberate Relationships' with Students

The central role of relationships with students is examined in detail in Chapter 4. Managing these relationships needs to be considered as a key factor in developing teaching expertise. It is surprising that little attention has been given to the need to reflexively examine these relationships. Tom (1997) uses the term 'deliberate relationships' to describe thoughtfully and deliberately creating a relationship in which students can learn and where over time teachers can support students' increasing ability to claim power. Her work is underpinned by a concern with surfacing power relationships between faculty and students. Part of this deliberate relationship is 'transparency of practice' which involves: (1) explaining to students what we are doing – or what we think we are doing – and why we are doing it; (2) moving from unconscious or hidden norms of action to explicit establishment/negotiation of ground rules; and (3) analysing power dynamics. Two other concerns are that the needs of teachers be met (as well as students) and respecting the whole person, both student and teacher.

The three approaches that we have discussed as ways to support the development of university teaching expertise are all underpinned by the notion of reflexivity, self-monitoring and monitoring of relationships with others on a continual basis.

To conclude, given the situated nature of university teaching practice and the development of teaching expertise, there can be no universal enduring story of the development of teaching expertise, nor can there be a single model of what constitutes 'teaching excellence'. In developing their expertise teachers work with a range of understandings of teaching expertise and engage with these understandings in shaping their own teaching practice. Such understandings are given expression in educational theory and research, prevailing institutional values, the formulation of educational policies and public commentary on education. It is important for university teachers to appreciate such understandings as contested discourses that have particular historical, social and political origins and which find expression in everyday practices. It is the critical scrutiny of these practices that is the hallmark of teaching excellence.

Enhancing Professional Practice

Take some time out from your daily routine and write 1–2 pages about the story of your teaching life. If you are just commencing your university teaching career you may wish to interview an experienced teacher and document their story.

When you read the story you have written consider the following questions:

1. What life experiences do you think have shaped your views on teaching and learning?
2. Do certain values you espouse about teaching come through in this story?
3. Where are your passions? What energises you?
4. How do you deal with disappointment and setbacks?
5. How would you like to be remembered by your students?
6. What steps do you take on a weekly and monthly basis to develop and sustain your teaching expertise?

CHAPTER 4

Framing Teacher–Learner Relationships

Introduction

Teacher–learner relationships are at the heart of teaching practice. Yet these relationships often remain unexamined. Continuing the theme of reflexive engagement, we explore in this chapter the influence of teachers' own educational experiences in framing teacher–learner relationships and the variety of ways in which teachers position themselves or are positioned in relation to their students. To add life to this discussion and give a sense of the emotions encountered in teaching, particularly in the early days, we draw on the experiences of award winning teachers who narrated their teaching life stories in a recent study conducted by one of the authors (McMullen, 2008).

We take the view that teaching practice involves much more than mastery of technical skills. It has a moral and relational dimension as highlighted by Noddings (2003), 'We affect the lives of our students not just in what we teach them by way of subject matter but how we relate to them as persons' (p. 249). There is nothing new in the suggestion that good teachers understand the need for caring relationships with their students. Carl Rogers in *Freedom to learn* (1983) highlights the role of relationships in creating a climate that enhances natural potentiality and desire for learning.

> The facilitation of significant learning rests upon certain attitudinal qualities which exist in the personal relationship between the facilitator and learner ... Here is a vital person, with conviction, with

feelings . . . She doesn't fit into some neat educational formula. She is, and students grow by being in contact with someone who really and openly is. (pp. 106–107)

However, given the intensification of work in contemporary universities there is a need for greater examination of the ways in which university teachers negotiate the multiple obligations they face and the emotional work involved in this negotiation process. Are the idealised relationships promoted by Rogers possible in today's higher education setting? As part of their relationships with students, teachers need to be aware themselves, and make their students aware, of the broader context within which their relationship takes place.

Our power is limited because we teach in a larger cultural, social and institutional context. We must not pretend – to ourselves or to our students – that we can single-handedly create classrooms that are immune to the pressures of these contexts.

(Tom, 1997, p. 15)

In most discussions of teacher–learner relationships, the focus is generally on student needs. It is also worth remembering the needs of teachers. 'As teachers we do have needs in the teaching relationship, and it is appropriate for them to be met in this relationship. We learn and grow with students: as they learn so do we' (Tom, 1997, p. 13). The rewards from teaching, both intellectual and emotional, often come predominantly from relationships with students.

Finally critical teachers need to be aware of the power dynamics that are ever present in relationships with students. In the final section of this chapter we address issues of power in teacher–learner relationships and introduce the concept of the 'deliberate relationship' as advocated by Tom (1997).

Past Experiences Shaping Ideals of Teacher–Learner Relationships

University teachers bring not just knowledge and skills, but also their individual biographies to the classroom. Memories of personal educational experiences can evoke strong emotions, both positive and negative, as well as clear views about types of learning situations and relationships to be encouraged or avoided. The way that teachers draw on their own experience can be conceptualised as assembling and deploying their own experience (du Gay, 1997) to shape their development as teachers including guiding their aspirations for developing relationships with students and avoiding the reproduction of negative experiences they remember as students. In making 'judgement calls' they draw on personal experience to inform their choices.

> I guess I have a unique set of experiences. But some of the elements I think a lot of teachers would have. And I think partly it's to do with having a natural propensity to want to help and assist and coach. . . . So there's a wider social, philosophical theme that sort of under-rides, underlies me, which is me as a person. It's through the various experiences I've had – it's a natural extension of me. And it appears now – a natural extension. It may not have been back then but it is now. And how it's helped me have, be confident enough to be able to drive into, to be successful in other areas as well. So yeah, so the whole concept of teaching and learning and stuff just infiltrates every aspect of my life.
>
> (John)

The narrated memories of early educational experiences form part of the picture of understanding the values that underlie teaching prac-tice. For some, it is painful learning experiences that have the most powerful impact on understandings of 'good teaching' and intentions for creating positive learning environments. Joy's perspective exemplifies this.

> The teaching I had never emphasised anything about me – that even though I did well in that system I didn't enjoy it . . . So a key for me has always been [to] know as much about my students as possible, as well as [to] know as much about the subject as possible so that I can make those things meet.
>
> (Joy)

For other teachers, changes in the higher education system mean that they feel unable to replicate the experiences and relationships that they fondly remember from their own student days.

> I certainly enjoyed the way my education was, when I did it in the wonderful days, where you had little tutorial groups of twelve. Twelve was a big tutorial and they expected you to read. And you didn't dare come in without reading and knowing and that was the way I did learn. I might have been pissed off some days when I didn't have time to do all the reading and then I lost marks but it was a wonderful discipline.
>
> [Now] you find that you can't discuss anything with anybody because nobody has read anything. And they all say they were working and they get angry because they see my role as standing

there, just putting data up on the board. 'We don't need to talk, just stick everything up there.'

(Sandra)

While individual teachers will have unique experiences that inform their teaching practice, we need to look beyond the individual's perspective. An individual's teaching practice is located in specific historical, social and cultural conditions. Thus the reflexive learning processes involved in teaching practice depend on communication and action with others because learning is embedded within societal structure and cultural contexts of interpretation (Alheit & Dausien, 2002).

When teachers discuss their teaching practice they represent themselves as particular types of teachers with identity being actively constructed through both 'sameness' and 'otherness', in a process of defining who they are in relation to others. They create a place and positionality for themselves within their universities, attempting to position themselves as 'knowers' in their own eyes as well as those of students, other academics and their institution.

This relational aspect of teaching is evident in Joy's story below. Her story cannot be told without reference to the other players in her story: her students, her colleagues and her institution. Central to this story is the changing dynamics in these relationships as she develops personal confidence in her expertise as a university teacher.

From Novice to Expert Teacher through a Relational Lens – Joy's Story

The journey from novice teacher to legitimacy as an expert teacher is charted in Joy's story. Joy completed her undergraduate studies in Australia before heading overseas for professional experience later followed by doctoral work at a North American university. It was as a doctoral student that she had her first teaching experience, which often involved team teaching with colleagues from a range of departments. Back in Australia she has been at her current institution for over 15 years teaching very large undergraduate classes as well as specialised postgraduate courses. She was a pioneer in her institution in the use of online learning.

What is evident in this story is the changing nature of Joy's relationships with her students as she develops as a teacher. Joy tells of struggle and mistakes as she attempts to become the kind of teacher that she aspires to be. She moves from fear and anxiety about being exposed as an impostor to having the confidence to empower her students. In analysing Joy's narrative and examining the ongoing self-work she engages in, we draw on the different ways of relating to oneself: knowing oneself, controlling oneself, caring for oneself and (re)creating oneself (see Tennant, 2005). These 'techniques of self', practices by which individuals seek to improve themselves, can be seen to play an important role in the development of teaching expertise.

A constant theme in the story of Joy's early teaching experiences is the fear of being exposed as a fraud. She is constantly assessing how her performance measures up to her perceptions of the ideal teacher. Monitoring herself, and coming to know herself, Joy readily identifies deficits in her teaching in the early days.

> When I first started the anxiety [it] would have been enough for me not to even know where my skin finished and [the class] began. Very vulnerable. And a lot of the over preparation and going to all lengths to cover all bases would have been to actually try to measure up to being the expert, while constantly entertaining being an impostor anyway.

Despite her hard work, Joy sees herself as an impostor. This is not an uncommon feeling for beginning teachers or for students. Brookfield (2006) uses the label of 'impostor syndrome' to describe teachers' concerns that they don't really deserve to be taken seriously because they are just muddling through trying to avoid 'disaster' and exposure of their perceived inadequacies. Their own teaching lives in no way measure up to their idealised image of what a university teacher should be and how they would perform. Many teachers would identify with the comments by Kets De Vries (1993, cited in Brookfield, 2006).

> These people have an abiding feeling that they have fooled everyone and are not as competent and intelligent as others think they are. They attribute their success to good luck, compensatory hard work, or superficial factors such as physical attractiveness and likeability. Some are incredibly hardworking, always overprepared. However, they are unable to accept that they have intellectual gifts and ability. They live in constant fear that their impostorous existence will be exposed – that they will not be able to measure up to others' expectation and that catastrophe will follow. (pp. 79–80)

Brookfield (2006) observes that many teachers experience the impostor syndrome at various times in their teaching careers, not just in the early days. He suggests that teachers who react to student evaluations by giving greater emphasis to negative comments and discounting positive ratings are displaying impostorship. Departing from our comfort zones to experiment with new ways of teaching can also engender fears of looking foolish and not in control. Taken to extremes this anxiety can be crippling for both students and teachers. Brookfield (2006) advises that when impostorship is named as an everyday experience it loses its power, becoming a common feeling rather than a shameful secret. Being involved in team teaching or having a strong peer network can help to keep concerns in perspective. However, used in a mindful way these feelings can curb complacency and provoke us to see our teaching practice as being in a state of constant refashioning – both responding to and shaping our interactions with students.

Joy describes her experiences of 'impostorship' in this way:

> Having a sense as though everybody knew more than I did. And then being really quite shocked and surprised that they didn't. [Thinking] everybody's going to be able to see I am the impostor . . . somebody must have made a huge mistake . . . I'm not a teacher yet you know . . . So I think, you know, there was always that working hard to overcome the [feeling] everyone's going to detect it and I shouldn't be here. And that continual surprise about lasting.

Organisation and subject content were initially her key concerns and criticism from students was a key factor playing on her mind.

> The sole purpose of teaching well was in the fear of student evaluations. Like what they say about me is going to be so important. If they say I'm not organised or I'm not fair or biased, then that's going to be really, really terrible. Awful.

She tells of a focus very much on the subject matter, slavish with the content, rather than considering the students she was teaching. Her main focus appears to have been achieving her aspiration of positioning herself as subject expert.

> I think as a beginning teacher I would have been so good, at trying to keep it all the same and not make any modifications, as though the thing that I learnt in the book was more important than the people I was teaching . . . I think as a beginning teacher I was so nervous and anxious and that all the time, that I wouldn't have been, I wouldn't have had the better communication skills that we need as a teacher. That I would probably prepare about the *stuff* or the competence rather than for the *whom*. I think probably my timing would have been out, the rhythm of teaching, the listening to the students. Even though I used to ask them things.

In her early days of teaching Joy was very conscious of how her students would see her:

I think when I was a beginning teacher I would think about what I was going to wear and how I was going to look so that I would be that person they would expect to see. Whereas now I think I could teach in my pyjamas and I don't think it would make all that much difference. So I think you know that's not what matters anymore. So it's sort of more just getting that communication going really well.

Joy estimates that it took around five years to gain mastery in her teaching:

So I've probably got better at it over about 5 years. It took me at least that long to not think with a focus, so I'd get one thing right and then over commit in something else, and then 'Oh drat'. And so, to get the flexibility sort of took much longer I think. But I think after 5 years I was pretty much OK and running. It was more the first two years where I found that I used up a lot of energy and it was very bad to be young, yeah.

As she gained confidence Joy increasingly shifted her focus from the subject content to interacting with her students. The story below reflects her increasingly relaxed relationship with students while reinforcing her 'enterprising self'.

I would ask them to be in touch with me and of course on email they can be in touch with you any time day or night so they don't actually appreciate the fact that lecturers have lives. So if I was there and something came through I would just answer it straight away and so I got some nicknames that were kind of fun 'Duracell' (laughter) like the Duracell bunny because I would be kind of working around the clock. When work came in I'd just send it straight back. So students liked that. Students also then start keeping records to see who gets the prize for getting a response at the most ungodly hour of the night (laughter) . . . The Duracell bunny alerted me to the fact that it was better to answer their things in reasonable hours than when they come in even if I am up at 3 o'clock in the morning not to let them know that (laughter).

Despite having difficult times in her early teaching days, Joy talks throughout her story of being aware of the need to care for herself. This involved practices such as going for a drink with friends, keeping her sense of humour or easily forgiving herself.

Over time, Joy (re)creates herself as a teacher, reworking her identity from that of subject expert to someone who empowered students, helping students use knowledge as a way of getting on in the world.

> I guess letting go of the know-it-all was important. And taking up, not just a philosophy that people have to learn, but actually knowing that they do and they do everyday . . . Then me as teacher, I want the expert voice to actually be taken from me and given over . . . So yeah my expertise would definitely be in not being needed as someone to answer questions, but someone to consult on the best way to go about getting there. And also to actually be part of the audience that celebrates somebody's growing awareness, and the beauty of words. So I'm sure that that's pretty central to my idea of teaching . . . So the final product for me is empowering the student, watching the student see that knowledge is a way of getting on in the world and being more able to make decisions.

Talking about the influences on her teaching Joy draws connections between teachers she admired and her own teaching practices:

> I admire those teachers who actually said I could do something rather than 'I'm an expert and tell me how many reasons why'. And so the best teachers to me have been those who have walked their talk as I say and have actually succeeded on their own merit and they haven't really required me to shine the torch for them yeah. So I try, I don't even try, I just assume that the students are going to take off and be brilliant you know, I wouldn't have accepted them into the programme if I didn't believe in them (laughter) yeah and so yeah and to be here for when they have the troubles and things like that. To always be approachable and yet build some boundaries so that they don't gobble me up – which they don't do. Yeah, they're very, very respectful my students.

While, on one hand, many university teachers such as Joy understand themselves in terms of excellence and enterprise, they are exposed to the competing discourses of efficiency and quality assurance. Drawing on the discourse of managerialism and responding to the effects of massification in universities, university teachers are constantly being urged to 'do more with less'. Joy talks of the conflicts she experiences and the ways she works through these, either by resisting university efficiencies (at personal cost) or by developing new teaching strategies in some form of compromise.

> So I'm not a good teacher when it comes to how teaching is regulated. I really do think I just prefer to take the time . . .
>
> Practising what I preach . . . is often at variance to the university policy. So the University will be saying actually if you could do a two-hour lecture and one-hour tuorial that would really help out with accommodation and with casual staff and all sorts of things. So I was

interested not only in what the ideal situation is but also if I am going to have large classes how do I make those effective.

University teachers seem to be confronted with a paradoxical situation. In times when flexibility is being exhorted, there is the threat of a narrowing of identity options for academics as powerful and prescriptive imperatives emerge to satisfy the demands for accountability in universities. While the measurement of performance in universities may be contested, its influence is not likely to abate. Increasingly performance measurement will be a factor shaping institutional understandings of what it means to be a 'good teacher' and this will have flow-on effects for teaching practice and construction of university teachers' identities.

With the intensification of work in universities we believe there is a need for greater examination of the ways in which university teachers negotiate the multiple obligations they face and the emotional work involved in this negotiation process. In times of change, when teachers are faced with heavy workloads and competing demands, the quality of teacher–learner relationships can be an important factor in sustaining and re-energising university teachers.

Teacher–Learner Relationships and Care of Self

Good teaching experiences are charged with positive emotions of joy, excitement, elation and satisfaction. Bad teaching experiences can engender frustration, anger, disillusionment and despair. Emotions are central to teaching. Hargreaves (1998) drawing on a study of emotions and teaching in Canadian schools makes the comment below. It could equally be applied to university teachers:

> Teachers' emotional connections to students and the social and emotional goals they wanted to achieve as they taught those students shaped almost everything they did, along with how they responded to changes that affected what they did. Teachers wanted to become better so they could help their students more effectively. The emotional bond that teachers had was central to how they taught them. (p. 845)

In a recent study of award winning teachers (McMullen, 2008), there was rarely an instance where teachers spoke about their teaching without reference to the students involved. Discussion was not around 'I did this' or 'I did that'. Rather it was about what teachers did and how students responded or that students had particular needs, concerns or difficulties and particular teaching practices were necessary.

Care was the defining theme when Carolyn was asked how she would like to be remembered as a teacher. It was also her desire for that caring attitude to be reciprocated. She wanted to be remembered as:

> Somebody who cared about their subject and their students and their professionalism. Somebody who had integrity and authenticity. Somebody who was real. Somebody who the students actually cared about.
>
> (Carolyn)

Students' entitlement to respect and dignity is a given for Joy. Listening to students and affirming their world underpins much of her teaching practice.

> One of the things that I liked to do for the students is provide a structure and culture for them to thrive in. And also extend an attitude of respect and dignity. So that I don't ever say what they can't do, but I try and build on strengths.
>
> (Joy)

> I just have a great feeling that you have to be optimistic and you have to give people hope and also sort of allow them integrity, like to integrate what it is that's going on for them, and to listen to them.
>
> (Joy)

Work such as that of Connelly and Clandinin (1990), Elbaz (1991), Thomas (1995) and Nias (1996) explores the emotional qualities of teaching. Yet as their work draws predominantly on philosophical, psychological and literary foundations they tend to treat teachers' ways of knowing as mainly personal matters of moral choice, commitment and responsibility. 'This has been at the expense of considering how sociological, political and institutional forces shape and reshape the emotional landscapes of teaching for good or ill, in different ways under different conditions' (Hargreaves, 1998, p. 836).

Guilt, Hargreaves (1994) suggests, is a key feature in the emotional lives of teachers and others who work in caring professions. He sees teacher guilt as much more than a private trouble. He argues that it is socially generated, emotionally located and of practical consequence. He identifies four paths leading to teacher guilt: commitment to goals of caring and nurturance, the open-ended nature of the job, the pressures of accountability and intensification and the persona of perfectionism. All four factors are present in the stories told in McMullen's (2008) study of award winning university teachers. For example:

There is so much stuff I now just don't do because I can't do it because it's not humanly [possible] with the sort of numbers because of the time constraints and some of them – I think it's quite tragic.

(Carolyn)

One of the sad things is that you don't have the time . . . and so I probably make as many mistakes as the next one, but I try to limit that. And I don't think universities now – are really building into the workloads what it really takes to teach well.

(Joy)

Teachers respond in different ways to these structural constraints. There are risks of 'burnout', cynicism and exit from the profession. For Joy there is a balancing act in being approachable and protecting herself.

To always be approachable and yet build some boundaries so that they don't gobble me up – which they don't do.

(Joy)

The concept of 'emotional labour' (Hochschild, 1983) is also relevant to university teaching. Emotional labour describes the work of those employed in service sectors to project the expected emotions in their professional interactions. With teaching, emotion can be positive in terms of creating a sense of excitement and energy. However, it can also have negative consequences in situations of work intensification where a person identifies too wholeheartedly with the job and risks burnout (Hochschild, 1983). Emotional labour can take a toll on teachers where the projected emotions are manufactured. Here the teacher may engage in self-blame about this insincerity and experience cynicism and detachment.

But emotional labour is also the source of the greatest satisfaction. It is the strength of teacher–learner bonds that often serves to sustain and re-energise teachers.

the very positive energy that I got back from people when I was teaching. In other words, learning that I'm valued, people respect me and value me as a member of society.

(John)

Relationships are also a significant feature when teachers in McMullen's (2008) study talked about change in universities. They generally spoke of change in terms of how it affected students and how it affected their relationships with students.

Managing these relationships needs to be considered as a key factor in developing university teaching expertise. Given the central importance of the teacher–learner relationship, Tom (1997) advocates that it should be framed as a 'deliberate relationship' to signify that it has been thoughtfully and deliberately created. She describes it in this way:

> As a teacher I am creating a relationship in which students can learn. Thus my actions as a teacher are done on purpose and for a purpose. The deliberate relationship is a consequence of my awareness of acting in a relationship for a specific purpose. (pp. 12–13)

In the following section we examine in detail issues of power and what is involved in creating a 'deliberate relationship' with students.

Dealing with Power and Creating 'Deliberate Relationships' with Students

Self-monitoring and monitoring of relationships with students are ongoing activities in teaching practice, the development of teaching expertise and the fashioning of teacher identity. The term 'deliberate relationships' is used by Tom (1997) to describe thoughtfully and deliberately creating a relationship in which students can learn and where over time teachers can support students' increasing ability to claim power. Her work is underpinned by a concern with surfacing power relationships between faculty and students.

Tom identifies two common responses to relationships of power imbalance such as those between teachers and students. These are the response of *distance* and the response of *denial*. The response of distance is often formally embodied in professional codes of ethics setting out prescribed roles with a focus on public and formal discharge of roles. While this response acknowledges power and makes it visible it increases the privilege and sense of mystique associated with powerful positions and does not adequately support students' efforts to grow and negotiate changes in teaching relationships.

The response of denial is a more complex response where teachers attempt to minimise power differentials between themselves and students in an attempt to equalise or disavow power imbalances. Tom argues that the response of denial sets up a set of complications and contradictions. Teachers have come to realise that the power teachers hold by virtue of their expertise and institutional roles is something that they must own and use responsibly rather than disavow, 'if we are to truly teach we must acknowledge and use the power of our position' (Tom, 1997, p. 11). While many student-centred teachers are uncomfortable with the idea that they are the focus of attention in the classroom, Brookfield (2006) cautions that this will always be the case where a teacher holds the power of the grade and the focus should be on using your power to the best effect. To pretend that you don't have power, he suggests, will only cause students to be suspicious and damage trust in the classroom.

Attempting to substitute a frame of 'friendship' or equality for the relationship of teaching can often result in a situation that meets the needs of the teacher rather than students (Tom, 1997). While students like to know their teachers have a life outside the classroom they dislike what they perceive as inappropriate disclosures about their private life (Brookfield, 2006).

Rather than responding to power with distance or denial Tom (1997) advocates the thoughtful and deliberate creation of relationships with students. This deliberate relationship reflects a reflexive awareness of acting in the relationship for a specific purpose. 'Transparency of practice' plays an important role in the relationship and involves: (1) explaining to students what we are doing – or what we think we are doing – and why we are doing it; (2) moving from unconscious or hidden norms of action to explicit establishment/negotiation of ground rules; and (3) analysing power dynamics. This is designed to occur in a context where needs of students and teachers are met and there is respect for the whole person, both student and teacher.

Enhancing Professional Practice

Think about the very first session of a programme you teach. The very first time you interact with students either in a classroom setting or online. What happens and what are the consequences of that first encounter?

In this chapter we have argued for the importance of establishing relationships with students in a deliberate way. Focusing on that first encounter take some time and reflect on the following issues:

1. What rules are being established either from a course or institutional perspective in that first session? What issues of power can you observe in this interaction? How comfortable are you with these rules? Do you find them constraining (and in what way) or do they align well with the values that underpin your teaching practice?
2. What aspects of etiquette are important to you in the classroom? Some examples could be: students arriving after the class has started, talking in class, having mobile phones ring during class, students sending text messages. What bothers you and why? What things don't worry you at all? Compare your list with some other colleagues and discuss differences in the things that concern you. Do you feel that some of the things that annoy you reflect on how you

think students are positioning you as a teacher? You may also want to reflect on these issues in an online learning environment.

3. How do you want to position yourself in relation to students? For example, it may be as a subject expert, an open and approachable teacher, 'tech savvy', someone who creates interesting and unexpected moments in class, a well-prepared and professional presenter, a teacher who expects high standards of their students or any combination of a range of positionings. Does this vary with different groups of students depending, for instance, on their stage of study? What do you do to help to position yourself in this way or do you just let it happen?

4. Are there additional factors that you will now consider the next time you take a class for the first time?

Learning Groups

Most books and manuals on teaching in higher education contain a section on how to manage and utilise groups for learning (see, for example, Exley & Dennick, 2004; Griffiths, 1999; Jaques & Salmon, 2007). Typically they focus on the various ways in which small groups can be assembled for the purposes of learning, varying from short-term informal in-class groups to check on understanding or to provoke group discussion or comment, through to the establishment of more formal learning groups that may span several weeks to carry out an experiment, write a report or carry out a project. These strategies normally involve breaking down a larger group into smaller groups – largely with the aim of providing scope for students to be more involved. The format of a large lecture followed by smaller groups working in tutorials or seminars has a long tradition in higher education, as does laboratory work and other practical classes. Groups are said to promote more effective learning, through shared support and mutual feedback (Davis, 1993). They generate the experiential base for learning, and they encourage interaction, self-determination and trust. Ultimately, it is only through the group that 'learning how to learn' can be achieved. It is not surprising then that much attention is given to the design and management of groups in higher education.

Much of what can be found in the higher education literature contains good practical advice on the design of group tasks and the management of groups. Griffiths (1999), for example, identifies an exhaustive list of small group teaching methods such as brainstorming, buzz groups, cross-over groups, fishbowls, peer tutoring, problem-based tutorial groups, simulations, role plays, games, seminars, syndicate groups and so on (see also Jaques & Salmon, 2007). Most of the advice on how to structure groups is based on the experience of teachers. While this is legitimate and valuable, the advice is rarely informed by research and scholarly work on groups. This work has emerged from a range of disciplines in the social and behavioural sciences, including psychology, management, sociology, political science and communication. The purpose of this chapter is to provide an overview of this scholarly work on groups and to analyse it from the point of view of how it can inform the practice of teaching in higher education.

A basic premise in small group research and theory is that a group is more than a mere collection of individuals, that is, groups have their own dynamic quite independent of the individuals comprising them. Understanding this dynamic and the practical implications is at the heart of our interest as educators. However, as mentioned above, understanding the dynamics of small groups has applications to other areas apart from education – in fact it is relevant wherever people need to work together to achieve a shared goal. Given the variety of practical applications of small group work it comes as no surprise to find that there are a diversity of theoretical perspectives and research traditions. One attempt to bring together in one place the variety of approaches to understanding groups is that of Poole, Hollingshead, McGrath, Moreland and Rohrbaugh (2004). This is a good starting point for what follows. Table 5.1 below sets out the focus and key features of each of nine perspectives identified by Poole et al. (2004).

Table 5.1 Interdisciplinary Perspectives on Small Groups

Perspective	Focus	Key features
Psychodynamic	Groups can be understood in terms of the psychodynamics in operation.	'The history of the group and its members, particularly unresolved problems or projects . . . leader-member dynamics revolving around dependence, independence, interdependence, and counterdependence; member attempts to position themselves in the group in order to address problems or needs; the development of group fantasies and group orientations such as fight, flight, and engagement behaviours . . .; member and group growth and development and satisfaction of member and group needs' (p. 7).

Functional	Focus is on the factors that influence group effectiveness – assumes that groups are goal oriented.	'The nature of the group's task, the internal structure of the group, group cohesiveness, group composition, and the group's environment . . . group effectiveness as measured by productivity, efficiency, and quality; leadership effectiveness; and satisfaction with the group outcomes' (pp. 7–8).
Temporal	Focus is on how groups develop and change over time.	Stages and phases of group development. Processes leading to changes in the group (e.g. roles, leaders, effectiveness, goals).
Conflict-power-status	This perspective 'examines groups in terms of the dynamics of power, status, resources, and social relationships and the group structures associated with these processes' (p. 8).	Inequalities among members in terms of resources, status, and power. How these inequalities are generated and reproduced and how they influence group processes and outcomes, conflict management, negotiation, consensus building and distribution of resources.
Symbolic-interactionist perspective	This perspective 'focuses on the social construction of groups and offers explanations based on the meaning that groups have for their members' (p. 9).	Social interaction, language, symbols, and individual and collective interpretative schemes . . . Progress towards outcomes related 'to symbolic-interpretive processes, such as a common vision, group identity, internal group structures and group boundaries, as well as effectiveness, group cohesion, and member satisfaction' (p. 9).
Social identity	This perspective 'examines groups in terms of members' sense of the social groups they belong to, their identification with these groups, the social identity they construct based on this identification, and the dynamics between in-groups and out-groups driven by social identity' (pp. 9–10).	'Key processes include self-categorization, depersonalization, inclusion/exclusion, social influence, stereotyping, and intergroup conflict. Member self-concept, group cohesiveness, loyalty, turnover, conformity, and social loafing' (p. 10).

(Continued overleaf)

Table 5.1 Continued

Perspective	Focus	Key features
Social evolutionary	'This perspective posits that group structure and interaction reflect evolutionary forces' (p. 10).	'People (or in some cases, the cultures in which people live) have inherent tendencies toward group behaviour that have evolved because they increase the likelihood of survival and reproduction. Processes and outcomes are influenced by these tendencies' (p. 10).
Social network	This perspective 'considers groups as interlinked structures embedded in larger social networks. Groups, their properties, and their processes are conceptualized in terms of patterns of relationships among members' (p. 10).	'Processes within networks include affiliation, exchange, influence, information flow, diffusion, and reticulation of the network. Key outcomes include task effectiveness and efficiency, cohesiveness, attitude and belief convergence, and change in the network . . . how patterns of relationships between members affect functioning at the group level' (p. 11).
Feminist	This perspective challenges traditional approaches by 'investigating and theorizing how power and privilege are enacted through interactions that favour one gender over another' (p. 11).	'traces group dynamics and outcomes to differences in male and female motivations in social situations, their views of groups, and their different life experiences. There is an assumption that typical social structures and conditions are tilted toward male standpoints and privilege them over female views, although participants are generally unaware that this is the case. The result is a tendency by both researchers and groups to emphasize rational, task-focused concerns over relationships and community' (p. 11).

Source: After Poole et al., 2004

Each of the above perspectives brings with it different assumptions about groups and has a different focus. For example, the psychodynamic perspective assumes that deep psychological dynamics underlie the surface behaviours of groups, and so the focus is on the affective and emotional aspects of groups; the functional perspective starts from the assumption that groups are goal oriented and so the focus is on group behaviours that promote effective performance; the temporal perspective assumes that groups change and develop over time, and so the focus is on stages of development and factors promoting change; and so on. Despite these differences there are some common observations that can be made about groups that are relevant to all perspectives. These are set out by Jaques and Salmon (2007) and presented below in an edited and tabulated version.

Table 5.2 Properties of Groups that are Common to Different Perspectives

Properties of groups	Questions to pose about properties
Time boundaries	How well were the members prepared for joining the group? What are their expectations about the group and their role in it? Should there be any rules about openness and confidentiality? What prior experience of group work have they had?
Physical environment	What associations does the room have for the group members? Can everyone be equally spaced? Is the space flexible? Does anyone have a special position?
Group size	What size of group is appropriate to the aims? Will the group be large enough with one or two absences?
Group composition	What are the main differences between members? How can the range and balance of roles and expertise be predetermined? What kinds of tasks are suitable?
Participation pattern	How much of the talking is done by each of the members? To whom are questions or comments usually addressed? Are all members engaged in the discussion/task? Is non-verbal participation evident?
Communication	Are members listening to each other? Do they make connections to or build on each other's contributions? Does the leader (either formal or informal) dominate discussion? Are feelings as well as thoughts communicated?
Cohesiveness	How satisfied are members with the group and their part in it? Did members seem glad to see each other? Did members talk inclusively about the group (e.g. 'our group' and 'we')? Did members turn up on time and stay without being distracted? Was there a sense of shared purpose?

(Continued overleaf)

Table 5.2 Continued

Properties of groups	Questions to pose about properties
Norms	Was there a shared understanding of matters such as self-discipline, courtesy, tolerance of difference, responsibility, freedom of expression and the like? Are these norms well understood? Are there marked deviations from the norms and what is the group's response? Which norms help and which seem to hinder the group's progress?
Sociometric pattern	Which members identify with and support each other? Which members seem repeatedly at odds with others? Do some members' comments act as 'triggers' for others?
Procedures	How will the group decide on aims, tasks and agendas? How is the group to make decisions? What regular process problems are likely to arise? How are the procedures going to ensure full involvement? How will the group monitor and evaluate its performance?
Structure	What kind of group roles and functions exist (group building vs task roles) – what are missing? What role did the leader adopt – instructor, facilitator, chairperson, resource, consultant? Was the group structure invisible, visible, appropriate to the task?
Aims or goals	How involved were the members in the setting of goals and aims? Were these acceptable to them? What separate and independent aims did members have?

Most experienced teachers would recognise the features and properties being described in the above tables although they would not necessarily be familiar with the terms used. The kinds of questions posed provide a useful checklist for teachers, but to see them as a checklist only is too simplistic – most of the questions are very large and complex, and the actions a teacher should take after responding to the questions are not clear cut and involve significant judgement. For example, the question 'How is the group to make decisions?' goes to the heart of power relationships in the group and the role of the teacher in group life. This is not simply an educational question, it is a highly political question. Similarly, with the question 'What separate and independent aims did members have?' – this addresses a core issue in the humanities and social sciences concerning the relationship between individuals and the groups to which they belong. The question 'What are the main differences between members?' raises an important contemporary question about how to cater for diversity in the classroom. Diversity challenges the way in which shared goals and shared ways of working are approached. For example, group discussions are often based on certain assumptions about how people interact with each other and take turns, which is highly culturally specific. This means that teachers need to address this issue in an explicit way and not fall into the trap of assuming too much. The question 'How satisfied are members with the group and their part in it?' raises the issue of whether the group meets the needs of its members. This too raises the question of who should be in a position to judge the members' needs, or whether needs should be articulated and analysed prior to the group embarking on its task.

These questions clearly point to the political dimension of groups. They invoke other questions such as 'in whose interests is the group working?' and 'whose voice is being heard?' There is also a strong psychological and sociological dimension which has to do with feelings and behaviours such as attachment, identification, cohesion, conformity and relationship building. Teachers in higher education clearly need to address the likely political and psychological dimensions when using small group teaching strategies. The remainder of this chapter explores some of the issues in doing so.

The Individual/Group Tension in Education

Many of the goals of education are expressed as outcomes for individual students, after all it is the individual who passes or fails a subject and it is the individual who takes away a qualification at the end of their degree. To what extent then is the group the real focus of educational work? Is it simply seen as a vehicle through which individual achievement is fostered? This is likely to be the mindset of many teachers, especially those who subscribe to a humanistic conception of the value of education with its revered educational notions such as the dignity of the person, self-direction, self-development and autonomy – all of which place the individual at the centre of a value system which relegates the 'group' to second place. Symptomatic of this 'individualist' approach to groups is a conception of group work as a means to an end. The claim is that group learning is better than, say, the lecture format, because it encourages the pooling of resources, builds a sense of group believing, allows participants to express their views, helps them to clarify their thinking and so on. The educator's task is to develop an armoury of group teaching techniques, a sensitivity to the pitfalls of group work and an ability to intervene appropriately in the group process. The ultimate aim is to establish a smoothly functioning, cohesive group in which individuals can work together and learn productively. The group dynamics literature offers an abundance of supportive material on conformity, group cohesion, leadership, communication structures, the emergence of norms, group development, group decision making and individual versus group performance – all of which can be used in the service of understanding how the individual is influenced by the group or how a particular individual (the facilitator) can influence the life of the group.

But there is also an educational tradition which advocates a more communal approach to groups (see, for example, Brookfield, 2005). The communal approach is overtly political in the sense that it advocates the empowerment of certain groups in society such as the working class, peasants and women and racial, indigenous or religious minorities. It is also opposed to education initiatives which are solely used as vehicles for personal advancement, which, in the final analysis, will only produce 'clever rogues'. This commitment to the group originates from a political ideology which emphasises the importance of democratic leadership, participation in decision making, cooperative activities and self-management. The foundations for practice here are political and social theory, rather than social psychology or group dynamics. The idea of group self-determination is a political and moral imperative and the purpose of group work is not so much to promote group cohesion or arrive at some kind of consensus, as to provide a forum for democratic discussion and decision making.

These two approaches to the group are not necessarily antagonistic – in fact the best teachers are mindful of both the individual and communal aspects of group work, and are able to blend and balance individual and group achievement. A fundamental principle, however, is that groups simply do not exist if they have no power. The key decision for teachers then is how much power can be ceded to the group, given the constraints and structures in higher education.

At the outset it is important to ask under what conditions do we consider that a 'learning group' has been formed? For example, is a typical class that is brought together over a term or a semester a 'learning group'? In answering this question we need to ask whether there is a shared group goal, given that groups are most commonly thought of as two or more people working together towards a common goal. Is there a common group goal or are there simply individual goals (e.g. for each student to achieve a good grade)? In these circumstances the 'group' as such is an artificial construction – it does not emerge naturally from the motivations of the individual members. This means that teachers need to be mindful of how a group forms a sense of cohesion, how groups develop and build over time and how the dynamics of the group work to influence its members towards the goals the *teacher* has in mind. Such a scenario sees the teacher as taking on the key leadership role. While this is no doubt necessary in the initial stages of group formation, an eventual goal for most 'learner-centred' teachers is to meet the *group's needs* rather than their own needs and to provide a platform for group empowerment.

Groups are often seen as vehicles for enhancing learner participation in their own education – the rationale is that it is only through group methods that the true needs of the group can be surfaced and addressed. The idea of meeting needs, however, is not as straightforward as it initially sounds. There are those who reject the needs meeting paradigm as a legitimate approach to education provision (e.g. Armstrong, 1982; Griffin, 1983) claiming that it is no more than a slogan which only serves the interests of the professional providers. These commentators generally focus on the ideological workings of the needs concept and how it influences the broad sweep of education provision. But our concern here is with what 'meeting group needs' means for a teacher who is responsible for a group of learners and who has some notion that meeting their needs might be a good idea. The first difficulty this person will face is to distinguish between the needs, demands and wants of the group (see Wiltshire, 1973; Lawson, 1975; Tennant, 1985). Wants are normally considered to be desires, pure and simple, without any appraisal of the value of satisfying those desires. A demand is best thought of as the overt expression of a want: 'we would like to learn some fundamental theorems' or 'we want more time allocated to class discussion' are examples of direct demands. An indirect demand would be the number of people who drop out of the course. A need then is a 'want' or 'demand' which is deemed worthy of satisfying. Thus needs are not neutral – they require a judgement by someone about the relative merits of satisfying different wants or demands. Exactly how this judgement is to be made in a learning group is indeed problematic.

This scenario is further complicated by the contradiction of trying to meet both individual and group needs simultaneously. To assume that group needs are compatible with the interests of individual members presupposes a consensus which is rarely evident. Indeed, there is a necessary gap between the needs and interests of the group and the needs and interests of the individual. Every group at some stage infringes on individual autonomy and therefore a judgement must be made about a just or equitable arrangement for meeting the needs of the individual in the context of the group's needs.

One technique, the Nominal Group Technique (NGT), is arguably a good way to approach the two tasks of evaluating wants/demands and blending individual and group needs. The steps in this technique are outlined in Table 5.3.

Table 5.3 Steps in the Nominal Group Technique

1. The task is stated (e.g. what issues should this series of seminars address?).
2. Participants write down their ideas silently and independently.
3. All ideas are listed in 'round-robin' fashion with clarifying comments/questions but no discussion.
4. Ideas are defended by the proposer and agreements or disagreements are voiced.
5. Group members evaluate the ideas, list their top 5 priorities and then rank these priorities from highest (5 points) to lowest (1 point).
6. The vote is tallied and the results recorded on a flowchart.
7. There then follows further discussion of the ideas and the voting pattern.
8. The voting process is repeated, the ideas are tallied and then listed in rank order.

This technique has been designed to allow a balanced input from all group members, especially during the initial stages. It also preserves the anonymity of the voter thereby (presumably) reducing the pressure on the individual to conform to majority opinion. But it is a mechanical process which really only delays the issue at stake – what to do with the final list of ideas. Is the final list of ideas binding on all members of the group? Is it subject to revision? What are the conditions under which it can be revised? These questions indicate that in the NGT the neutrality of the seminar leader and the diminution of the group dynamics process are short lived. Sooner or later the group must start functioning as a group and not as a mechanical device for meeting needs or decision making.

There are many other techniques comparable to the NGT but they mostly amount to a set of rules for decision making or problem solving which function in a similar manner to 'standing orders' in a committee meeting (for example, the Delphi technique as described by Jaques and Salmon, 2007, p. 132). But this is rarely the most fruitful way to proceed in establishing group needs. The idea that a group 'need' is there at the start of a learning process is a mistaken one; as mentioned earlier, most learning groups are artificial in the sense that it is individuals who come to learn and the group only emerges when there is a recognition of interdependence. Using a mechanical technique at the outset as a method of programme planning will result only in an aggregation of individual needs – it will almost certainly fail to register the needs arising from the emerging interdependence within the group.

Promoting Group Cohesion

Teachers often refer to the desirability of group cohesiveness – which normally means the extent to which group members are attracted to the group. The positive consequences of group cohesiveness are well documented for experiential, learning and working groups, and group cohesion is often portrayed as an important step in the growth of groups towards maturity. Given this, it is understandable that group exercises have emerged which have as their primary goal the enhancement of group cohesiveness. Given also that cohesiveness is expressed in terms of the affective non-instrumental behaviour of the group, it is easy to see why such group exercises focus on the release of emotional tension, the breakdown of defences against learning, the enhancement of interaction among group members and so on. The value of working towards such goals is unquestionable. However, some of the exercises and techniques recommended in training manuals and practised in countless training and education workshops are of questionable value. The 'icebreaker', for example, is a familiar experience for most people involved in education. Like many experiential group techniques in education, its origins can be traced to the human potential movement and the techniques associated with it, such as 'T-groups' and 'encounter' groups (for recent reviews see Weigel, 2002; McCleod & Kettner-Polley, 2004). Some of the excesses of this movement were earlier documented by Malcolm (1975), who notes three key features of the exercises commonly used:

1. A focus on the immediate 'here-and-now' experience of participants.
2. A belief that individual change occurs more readily in groups.
3. A belief in the value of open, honest feedback and self-disclosure.

Malcolm's objection to these (exclusively) experiential exercises is that the individual, far from being enhanced, must surrender to the group will. In the typical T-group, which is an unstructured, essentially leaderless group that has as its purpose a fuller understanding of self and others, the rules governing the behaviour of participants are well known beforehand (despite disclaimers to the contrary). In Malcolm's account these rules operate very much against the individual. For example, the need to focus on the 'here and now' typically appears as an aggressive anti-intellectual attitude in the group, where the display of individual knowledge and expertise is invariably interpreted as a defence against the spontaneous expression of feelings. Those behaviours which are encouraged are those which are prohibited in the course of normal social interaction, at least in the population. Failure to accept 'honest' and 'open' feedback (which might mean some kind of abuse from another group member) is considered deviant, as is the failure to 'confess' one's true feelings, or worse still – not agreeing to participate in the activities of the group.

Malcolm makes a compelling case that the extreme elements of the human potential movement use techniques which are manipulative, demeaning and, because they are effective, quite dangerous. His case can also be applied to some experiential techniques adopted by educators, particularly those used as short cuts to establishing group cohesiveness such as the 'ice-breaker'. The typical icebreaker has all the ingredients of the human poten-tial 'experiential' exercise – it often involves some kind of childish game, it invariably requires group interaction on an emotional level and it demands some kind of self-disclosure. The following is an activity that is recom-mended at the beginning of a group working on communication, multi-cultural or interpersonal issues; it is called 'Insight by Surprise' (Luft, 2000). It is used to help people see others with fresh eyes, and to raise awareness of stereotypes. It begins with a group of people unknown to each other. They stand in a circle. One person is chosen by the facilitator to pick another person to form a second group, the two then choose another to join them, and so on until another group of equal size is formed. This group forms an inner circle and the inner and outer circles now face each other.

> The people in the inner group are asked to move around in a circle, slowly and silently, so they pass the members of the outer group, looking carefully at each person as they pass. . . . Then people in the inner circle are asked to choose someone in the outer circle who is different from them in every way they can think of . . . I then ask them to move toward and stand opposite the person whom they think is as different from themselves as possible. (p. 137)

There are some other elaborations but the point is made – it is an exercise which is deliberately ambiguous and potentially quite confronting. The discussion question recommended is: 'Well, so how did it go?' The progress of this exercise would very much depend on how it was introduced and the 'climate setting' of the leader prior to introducing it. However, it is a risky exercise, and one can imagine all manner of disastrous outcomes. One problem, for example, is that the activity is aimed at providing insight for one group only – the inner circle – the others are left 'on the outer' so to speak, being merely objects of assessment. Why were they not chosen to be in the inner circle? On what basis were they being described as different? How do they feel about their difference being highlighted and used by others to explore their assumptions?

Another frequently used icebreaker involves the teacher developing a list of characteristics, such as 'likes dogs' or 'is an only child' or 'has visited China' – the list may be, say, 10 items long. As each characteristic is read out the students physically place themselves to the right or left according to whether it is true of them (a variation is to place yourself along a con-tinuum). Now this can be a very energising exercise and it can achieve what it sets out to do – to start the process of group building. However, everything depends on the list that is developed. It is actually quite difficult to develop a 'neutral' list which does not have the potential to embarrass or exclude.

For the most part icebreakers are harmless games which, at the very worst, may be a little insulting to the participant's intelligence or capacity for social intercourse. But one should nevertheless be conscious of the dangers of using such exercises at the beginning of the group life. The individual at this point is likely to be more compliant and it is particularly difficult to opt for non-participation. Notwithstanding this, as the group develops, its power to produce conformity among its members is strengthened. For this reason teachers need to be particularly aware of any group exercises that have the power to produce conformity against the wishes of the participants. One of the authors learnt this lesson early in his career when he was facilitating a values clarification exercise in a course for adult educators. The exercise involved a hypothetical post-apocalyptic scenario whereby the survivors of a nuclear holocaust were asked to choose their fellow survivors from among a list of potential people with defined characteristics (e.g. young female, young male, doctor, engineer, etc.). This was a well-known exercise at the time and it was used extensively in the period when anti-nuclear marches were at their peak in western countries. The problem with this exercise is that it asks students to suspend their disbelief and accept what turned out to be outrageous for some of them – that survival and the possibility of a renewed life were actually possible after a global nuclear war. In some respects it was fortunate that some way into the exercise a small group refused to continue – a lively discussion ensued (with some painful exchanges) and the exercise was abandoned for another less controversial scenario.

It is possible to avoid situations like the above if some fundamental principles in using group experiential techniques are adhered to. These are:

1. The principle of informed consent, i.e. the participants should be told the precise nature of the exercise.
2. The principle of freedom to participate, i.e. participants should be free to leave the group at any time. Ideally this freedom means freedom from the group pressure to conform, which of course is something extremely difficult to eliminate. It is therefore a principle which needs to be strongly stated and frequently reiterated by the group facilitator.
3. The principle of critical reflection, i.e. making sense of the experience by analysing and evaluating it (see Boud, Keogh & Walker, 1985; Zeichner & Liston, 1987).

Earlier I argued that a great deal of group work in education is done in the name of individual growth and development. Paradoxically, one of the greatest dangers of group work comes from the power of the group to shape and maintain the behaviour and beliefs of its members. In this context a knowledge of group dynamics can best be used to ward off oppressive aspects of the group. This is a particularly important function for educators who constantly witness the transformation of collections of individuals into groups of one sort or another.

The Development of the Learning Group

The brief examples of group techniques in this chapter could be multi-plied. The point I wish to draw from them is that groups are not mechan-ical objects which can be manipulated by a skilled facilitator. The literature on group development confirms this view. In general it considers groups to be organic entities with characteristic and predictable patterns of growth and development. Arrow, Poole, Henry, Wheelan and Moreland (2004) describe five models for analysing the way in which groups change system-atically over time. There are variations within each model but a common concern across all models is how the group sorts out its authority, power and interpersonal relationships. This is well illustrated with respect to the Sequential Stage Model, where Arrow et al. identify a common pattern of five stages:

1. **Inclusion and dependency** – where there is anxiety, dependence on a leader and testing to find out the nature of the situation and what behaviour is acceptable.
2. **Conflict** – where the focus is on issues of power, authority and com-petition, often with confrontation with the leader and resistance to the task.
3. **Trust** – where there is open negotiation of roles, tasks and the division of labour.
4. **Task orientation** – this is the work stage where there are constructive attempts to complete the task.
5. **Termination** – this is characterised by emotionality, realised as either disruption and conflict or the expression of positive feelings.

This contemporary summation resonates perfectly with the much earlier description of Tuckman and Jensen (1977) who describe groups as moving through the stages of forming, storming, norming, performing and adjourning. Thus the group development process is a linear step-by-step progression from immaturity to maturity which occurs across a range of group types (natural groups, laboratory groups, training groups, therapy groups, etc.).

Most teachers who work with groups have a sense of the evolution of group identity and the fluctuations in group life which accompany this process. The group development literature is useful in that it helps teachers to interpret events occurring within the group. However, it is unclear how the teacher should respond to these events and intervene in the group process. The option most frequently discussed in the literature is to devise strategies for facilitating the group through its various phases. Jaques and Salmon (2007) summarise the various factors to consider when enabling group interaction in both face-to-face and online environments: factors such as group size, group membership, the lifespan of the group, the physical conditions or virtual environment in which the group interacts, the role the teacher plays in the group process, the ground rules under which the group operates, the students' capacity to participate in group activities and the various leadership interventions possible. In all these interventions the dominant concern appears to be how to distribute authority and power within the group. A fatal mistake in organising any learning group is to create an illusion of freedom in the group which in fact does not exist. For example, an orientation programme for a group of learners may be organised around their perceptions of what they want to learn and how they intend to accomplish their goals. The organisers may have designed the orientation to facilitate the process of group development. In doing so they may promise that authority and leadership will be vested in the group. But this is risky without acknowledging the non-negotiable parameters and constraints. Without such acknowledgement the freedom of the group will be eventually exposed as an illusion leading to understandable hostility among the group members. To interpret this hostility as simply the next phase of group development (disenthrallment with organisers) would be trivialising what would be more accurately interpreted as a predictable response to being deceived.

The above hypothetical scenario illustrates how group events need to be interpreted in terms of the context in which the group exists. Groups do not operate in a vacuum with their own internal logic and developmental timetable. The dynamics of a group reflect not only its level of maturity, but the external constraints operating on it. A change in these external constraints can have an effect on group dynamics which overrides any ongoing developmental process. To this extent any notion of group maturity is at best provisional.

To conclude, much of the educational literature on managing learning groups places too much emphasis on the craft skills of the group facilitator and too little emphasis on the dynamics of group formation and change, and on the political dimension of group work. Most teachers would acknowledge the importance of building a good climate for learning and fostering connections among the students. However, a highly cohesive and consensual group should never be seen as an end in itself, without at least posing the broader questions to be considered such as 'cohesion for what purpose?', 'cohesion at what price?' and 'cohesion in whose interests?' – questions which are often overlooked by teachers whose main focus is on managing the group rather than empowering the group.

Enhancing Professional Practice

Write a 2–3 page commentary on the group dynamics of a class you have taught. This may take the form of a retrospective analysis of a class that has ended or a diary of observations on an ongoing class. Use Tables 5.1 and 5.2 to frame your commentary. In particular please comment on various group phenomena such as participation, group roles, the cohesiveness of the group, group development, group conflict, emerging norms and so on. Once the commentary is completed address the issue of whether you would do things differently. Discuss your commentary with others.

CHAPTER 6

Teaching for Diversity

Introduction

The move towards mass higher education resulting in an increasingly diverse student population and the rise of internationalisation were key trends identified in the introduction to this book. But the contemporary interest in diversity has its roots in at least two other concerns. The first of these is the equity and social justice agenda of higher education: that those who have suffered from disadvantage should have access to higher education and be able to participate without feeling excluded. The second has to do with preparing students to work effectively in a global environment, that is, to work with a diverse range of people, both as fellow employees and as clients. An extension of this second concern is the necessity for businesses to have a diverse workforce in order to thrive in a global environment. In this chapter we examine the implications of diversity and internationalisation for the work practices of academics in the higher education sector. There are two main areas of focus for discussion: (1) developing the capacity to teach an increasingly diverse student population; and (2) teaching to promote an awareness of diversity among students.

When discussing diversity within the student body we are referring to both visible and invisible differences including language, age, gender, cultural background, sexuality, religion, attendance pattern, family responsibilities, work experience, learning preferences, physical ability and disability. Different students will come with different levels of preparation for traditional styles of university study – what Ball, Macrae and Maguire

(1999) call 'educational inheritance'. They may have different expectations and concerns, ask different questions, bring different perspectives and experiences to the classroom and respond differently to classroom activities. This should not necessarily be viewed as problematic. However, it means that educators need to be mindful of the assumptions that underpin their teaching practice and their interactions with students.

While difference and diversity present challenges for educators there is the possibility to use difference in a positive way rather than as a 'deficit' in students to be remedied or a source of conflict and frustration. By embracing and harnessing difference in the classroom we have the opportunity to create a rich learning environment in which all students feel valued and where their abilities, backgrounds and life experiences are both recognised and utilised. Central to this task is the notion of inclusiveness through the facilitation of participation and the enhancement of quality learning of all students including those who are vulnerable to exclusion. Here the focus is not on the categorising and labelling of students, rather it is on developing the capacity to understand and respond to learners' needs by creating an appropriate learning environment.

An awareness of creating inclusive learning environments for students has been heightened by the increasing internationalisation of higher education. International educational experiences include studying abroad, studying at a foreign educational programme or institution in a student's home country or enrolling in online courses offered in other countries. Internationalism, exchange between nation states, was historically enacted by universities as cross-border exchanges of knowledge and people. However, in recent times borderless education has been used to describe the growth of internationalisation as a commercial enterprise, with international fee-paying students providing a revenue source to replace declining public funds for higher education (King, 2004). International students can be seen as both a symptom of globalisation and a driver of globalising tendencies in higher education (Ryan, 2004), as well as a catalyst for the promotion of an internationalised curriculum in higher education.

Internationalisation of Curriculum

Growth in student mobility (actual and virtual), developments in flexible delivery and 'new knowledge markets' and cultural diversification have been catalysts for universities to develop a more thorough understanding of and strategies for the internationalisation of curriculum (Rizvi & Walsh, 1998). The 'internationalisation of curriculum' has become a key concern not just to cater for the needs of international students but also to prepare all students to engage as global citizens in a rapidly changing, culturally diverse global context. This dual concern is reflected in the OECD's Centre for Educational Research and Innovation (CERI) definition of international curricula as 'an international orientation in content, aimed at preparing students for performing (professionally/socially) in an international and multicultural context, and designed for domestic as well as foreign students' (OECD, 1994, p. 9).

With international education we see the intertwining of economic and cultural concerns as highlighted by Rizvi and Walsh (1998):

> Internationalised curriculum based on values of 'innovation', 'flexibility' and 'enterprise culture' is highlighted, as is the idea of the 'client focus' in which internationalised study is seen to foster an in-depth knowledge of conditions in that country, cultural understanding and sensitivity, and the capability to deliver products and services that are responsive to the needs of the client. (p. 8)

Yet Rizvi and Walsh argue that the location of intercultural and international education within a discourse of economic necessity is problematic. They warn that 'productive diversity' can easily be mistaken for its corporate rather than its ethical impulse. In addition, by constructing cultural difference merely as a resource, the ways in which difference is historically constructed and enacted within social and administrative relationships within universities are essentially obscured. They argue that:

> Difference is not something that is external to the university; a resource that students bring to the university. Rather, it is something that is constitutive of social relations within the university. It is constructed and enacted through the practices of curriculum. To view difference as simply an external factor to be taken into account in the construction of curriculum is to treat it in an instrumental manner, to regard it as involving a cultural formation that is somehow external to what goes on in the university . . .
>
> What this argument implies is that the relationship between curriculum and cultural difference needs to be reconsidered in a more dynamic, relational way, rather than in purely instrumental terms . . . Our problem is not that, in a global university, students are different, but that we find it difficult to 'read' difference. As a result, some differences are sometimes overlooked when they should not be and, on other occasions, they are made to make more of a difference than they must . . . In internationalising the curriculum what is needed is a practical understanding of how difference can be both self-ascribed and constructed by others to deal with it; how students construct their identities and how it might be possible for

curriculum to engage critically with their contingent and relational character. (p. 9)

By taking a critical perspective on difference in higher education we can move towards a greater awareness and understanding of the social and political dimensions of difference and evaluate our practice both in developing the capacity to teach an increasingly diverse student population and in teaching to promote an awareness of diversity among our students.

Thus from a critical perspective:

Internationalisation of curriculum is more than a response to emergent global conditions, it is a framework of values and practices oriented towards a heightened awareness and appreciation of the politics of difference as the basis for developing the necessary skills and literacies for a changing world. International curriculum is therefore about an engagement within and beyond spaces of learning. (Rizvi & Walsh, 1998, p. 11)

Developing an Inclusive Higher Education Curriculum

How do we judge whether our universities are inclusive? While the move towards mass higher education in the last few decades has provided much wider access to universities and a more heterogeneous student body, Skelton (1999) cautions that inclusion in higher education is about more than access. It is about the experience of that higher education, and that experience may be exclusionary. Exclusion through cultural norms and practices can occur in a myriad of subtle and complex ways. Higher education, however, implicitly produces and reproduces particular cultural forms through its practices and it excludes others.

Again we can look to curriculum as a way to engage with issues of access and inclusion. What type of person – and graduate – does an educational institution wish to promote? For Nunan, George and McCausland (2000) this is the starting point in exploring how inclusive education in universities might be achieved. They connect the qualities of graduates with particular views of citizenship and public good and examine how curriculum should be shaped to achieve these qualities. Underpinning their argument is the distinction between two different notions of inclusivity in higher education, one linked to liberal ideals, the other derived from critical approaches. The liberal view of inclusivity stresses increasing participation and success in higher education by individuals from groups in society traditionally excluded and the subsequent social and economic advantages that stem from that participation. Success is focused on benefits to the individual and achievement is judged in terms of enculturation and reproduction of traditional professional knowledge bases and practices.

They contrast this with a critical perspective on inclusivity that is concerned with successful participation that generates greater options for all people in education and beyond. This construction of inclusivity has as a focus not just the factors directly affecting access, participation and success but also the criteria for judging success, and by whom success is determined. This view is not just about the means of achieving equitable outcomes for particular groups – it is also integral to the professional outcomes of courses for all participants. That is, personal benefit while still important is seen as a less desirable outcome than a situation where all graduates operate in more inclusive ways for the betterment of society. Embracing a social justice perspective involves questioning at an institutional level about how to address inclusive values in the socially constructed knowledge of our curriculum and the social relations in teaching and learning.

Nunan et al. (2000, p. 71) highlight that 'curriculum is a cultural artefact as it represents a set of choices about what knowledge and values should ultimately be transmitted to preserve the community that holds those values'. In this way curriculum can be viewed as a lever for wider social change and a site for contestation around competing values and ideas.

> The defining characteristic of an inclusive curriculum promotes this pluralism within a rigorous intellectual environment – a climate of critical consideration. It does not exclude ideas and values on the sole basis that they are linked to gender, culture, class, or 'race' . . . When a university declares through a mission that it will strive to be inclusive, it is declaring a political and educational ideal manifest in an inclusive curriculum . . . one approach to improving inclusivity is to focus upon a set of outcomes – the qualities of graduates – and look to ways in which these are aligned with the values that lie behind inclusive education. (pp. 71–72)

This social justice perspective on curriculum sits uncomfortably alongside the current market-oriented environment in higher education. Where students see themselves as 'customers' and institutions are reliant on new income streams to compensate for declining funding, tensions can arise. These tensions, underpinned by the competing values and attitudes of various stakeholders, can be played out in the classroom.

> Students can also exert power, particularly if they are paying substantial fees for their courses and some may choose to create problems for particular teachers if they regard themselves as being unfairly treated.
> (Huddleston & Unwin, 2008, p. 86)

Perceptions of 'unfair' treatment can often reflect the varied values, backgrounds and concerns that a more heterogeneous student population brings to its educational interactions. Teachers in diverse classrooms need to be mindful of the emotionally laden nature of some of the issues that non-traditional students have faced in their lives. It is commonly the case that people from disadvantaged backgrounds are politically aware and are quite reasonably sensitive to any processes and use of language that excludes them or demeans them in any way.

In the following section we explore a range of ways to think about teaching and learning in diverse classrooms.

Developing Academic Practices to Suit Diverse Student Bodies

Having surfaced the broader issues around diversity and inclusive education we can discuss a number of pedagogical strategies to enhance teaching and learning in diverse classrooms. We will look now at two different perspectives on developing students' academic practices. First, we consider the social nature of learning and examine ways in which students can be supported to participate in academic communities. Second, by taking an academic literacies perspective, we look in more detail at student engagement with multiple discourses and multiple forms of texts in academic communities.

Academic Socialisation and Participation in Academic Communities

A common concern with students entering university is working out what is required in a new context, predominantly in regard to writing and engaging with academic discourse. This is particularly the case with an increasingly diverse student body where learners can feel anxious and 'lost' in a new, bewildering or threatening learning environment and respond by seeking explicit guidance which lecturers interpret as a requirement for 'spoon feeding' (Sambell, McDowell & Sambell, 2006). By framing these concerns and responses to them in terms of academic socialisation we can work towards developing a more inclusive academic environment for all students.

In thinking about teaching students from increasingly diverse backgrounds, Northedge (2003a) challenges the idea that provision of 'remedial' support is the appropriate response to widening participation in universities. This, he argues, casts non-traditional students as weak students in need of help to keep up with 'proper' students. Instead he proposes an emphasis on the sociocultural nature of learning and teaching, drawing attention to learning as developing the capacity to participate in the discourses of an unfamiliar knowledge community and teaching as supporting that participation.

If students now vary significantly in what they bring to a course and what they need from that course, conceptualising teaching as transmission of knowledge in the form of information is unsustainable. As Northedge (2003a) observes:

> With a diverse student body, no fixed start or end point can be assumed, and consequently no selection of items can be appropriate to the needs of all. The challenges of diversity demand a more fluid conception of teaching. (p. 19)

Drawing on the work of Wenger (1998) and others he articulates the value of attending to the social nature of learning and emphasises that what students gain through a university education is the ability to participate in prestigious and powerful knowledge communities. Given the complexity and specialist nature of these communities, there are potentially many levels of participation. Northedge (2003a) identifies three levels:

- Central versus peripheral. Around the centre, well-established members participate in high-status communal activities while other members may be participating in more routine activities from the sidelines.
- Generative versus vicarious. This reflects the idea that in any discursive forum some take a 'generative' role in shaping the flow of meaning while others participate vicariously experiencing by listening or reading.
- Convergent versus variant understanding. This relates to the idea that while meaning is shared, understanding of what is said is not identical. Here a key function of discourse is to share knowledge between people who understand differently.

Applying these various levels to a diverse student entering a knowledge community, Northedge (2003a) outlines that:

> A student's goal is to become an effective participant in an unfamiliar knowledge community. The early stages will involve peripheral and vicarious participation with variant understanding. However, as the students' understanding becomes more convergent and as they acquire skills of generative participation, they gradually become able to participate more centrally. (p. 21)

The starting point for this journey is human experience from within the class or from resources such as case studies. This enables students to participate in shared meaning that in the initial stages of participation is based on the level of experience and understanding they bring to the educational setting.

A significant feature of Northedge's work on diversity and inclusion is the emphasis he places on the role of the teacher, a role that he warns can be relegated in the discourse of student-centred learning. Students need teachers, he argues (2003b), because:

> The teacher, as a speaker of the specialist discourse, is able to 'lend' students the capacity to frame meanings they cannot yet produce independently. (p. 172)

Expanding on the teacher's role as subject expert, he suggests that teachers have:

> three key roles in enabling learning: lending the capacity to partici-pate in meaning, designing well planned excursions into unfamiliar discursive terrain and coaching students in speaking the academic discourse. (p. 169)

He argues in particular of the dangers in the uncritical embrace of student-centredness if this results in an undermining of the role of the teacher and a downplaying of the contribution of the academy and academic knowledge.

> It is necessary that they [teachers] develop skills in being 'student-centred' but at the same time they need to speak as subject experts and take the lead in the teaching/learning process. To be 'student-oriented' is absolutely necessary, but not sufficient. The teacher's capabilities as subject expert are a resource vital to their students' progress. Failure to recognize this leads to weak, unfocused teaching. (p. 170)

What is at issue here is critical engagement by teachers with the relative positioning of teachers and learners in particular contexts and ongoing awareness of the varying contribution of multiple sources of knowledge. Northedge concludes that:

> HE [Higher Education] needs neither teachers who spout know-ledge endlessly, nor teachers who set their own knowledge aside for fear of distorting students' learning experience. Rather it needs teachers who know how to use their academic knowledge to guide and support bands of diverse students as they learn to participate in unfamiliar knowledge communities and acquire usage of their powerful discourses. (p. 179)

Whilst Northedge's work draws attention to the social nature of learning and the important role of teachers guiding students into university com-munities of learning, concerns have been raised that this 'academic socialisation' perspective fails to acknowledge the multiplicity of communities of practice within the academy and appears to assume that students are acculturated unproblematically into the academic culture though engaging with the discourses and practices of existing practitioners (Lea, 2004). Work on academic literacies provides a perspective that engages with issues of language, power, identity and what counts as knowledge.

Academic Literacies

In promoting the adoption of an academic literacies approach to course design Lea (2004) highlights that:

> The work on academic literacies argues that the relationship of students to the dominant literacy practices and discourses of the academy is more complex than other work on understanding student learning might suggest. That is, students are active participants in the process of meaning-making in the academy, and central to this process are issues concerned with language, identity and the contested nature of knowledge. (pp. 741–742)

Lea (2004) argues that, as reading and writing literacies are cultural and social practices they will vary depending on the context in which they occur. This adds to the complexity of negotiating the gaps between teacher and student understandings of writing for assessment. She highlights the value of a literacies approach for its capacity to draw attention to the increasingly different types of texts that students will engage with and the various types of knowledge addressed in these texts.

To date most of the research in this area of academic literacies has focused on the product produced by the student, for example, the essay or similar assignment. However, Lea (2004) makes the case for attention to be paid to a much broader range of the texts that students engage with in their study. This could include course materials, guidance notes for students, web-based resources, feedback sheets or even policy documents concerned with quality assessment procedures.

A literacies framework provides the opportunity for teacher and students:

> to collaboratively investigate the range of genres, modes, shifts, transformations, representations, meaning-making processes, and identities involved in academic learning within and across academic contexts. These understandings, when made explicit, provide greater opportunities for teaching and learning, as well as for examining how such literacy practices are related to epistemological issues.
>
> (Lea & Street, 2006, p. 376)

A detailed discussion of how a literacies approach has been implemented in a range of university subjects can be found in Lea (2004) and Lea and Street (2006).

Haggis (2006) argues that teachers in diverse classrooms need to be able to identify problematic aspects of higher education discourse and practice. Instead of attempting to offset the deficiencies of students through remedial work, they should at least pose the question 'what are the features of the curriculum, or of processes of interaction around the curriculum, which are preventing some students from being able to access this subject?' (p. 526). Take plagiarism as an example, which has been a topic of considerable debate within higher education worldwide in recent years. It is largely, although not exclusively, debated in the context of international students whose prior education has not highlighted the issue of plagiarism. When such students enter university they will very quickly encounter rules and regulations about the acknowledgement of sources and appropriate referencing styles. Yet this may often be a site for confusion and anxiety. A diverse range of factors can help explain why students plagiarise, including: confusion or ignorance about correct acknowledgement procedures; misunderstanding of western academic conventions; limited English language skills; and inappropriate assessment design.

As inclusive educators we can reflect on three key questions in relation to plagiarism. First, how do we see ourselves positioned in regard to plagiarism issues? Do we imagine ourselves as 'police' detecting academic misdemeanours, collecting evidence and preparing the case for disciplinary action? Second, do we see ourselves as educators with our focus on helping develop student awareness and skills that decrease the likelihood of 'intentional' or 'unintentional' plagiarism? Or, finally, do we adopt a less rule-bound and more flexible interpretation of plagiarism depending on the circumstances with which we are presented?

The framing and enacting of plagiarism rules and regulations is clearly an ongoing problematic in higher education. Our concern with the correct attribution of sources partly rests on the idea that students are expected to have their 'own voice' as demonstrated by their capacity to synthesise material from a variety of sources in an original 'line of argument'. Thus the student's voice and the voice of others need to be clearly demarcated in order to identify the 'contribution' that the student is making to the argument. But this tradition, which is exemplified in the 'essay', is not one universally known. Moreover, current debates about worthwhile knowledge point to the need for different kinds of assessments – ones where the issue of attribution is not as important.

Our aim in this section has been to draw attention to the complex and specialist nature of academic communities and the difficulties students can encounter when entering them. While many students find academic practices mysterious the potential for confusion and anxiety can be more pronounced for students from non-traditional backgrounds. By considering ways to make our educational environments more inclusive we can try to ensure that student energy is more keenly focused on positive aspects of learning and less on trying to work out and progress their way through an academic maze.

Finally it is worth restating that for both students and teachers an awareness of and capacity to engage with difference, both obvious and more subtle, and respond in a considered and respectful manner is an important part of contemporary life.

Enhancing Professional Practice

When we aim to connect with our students a common strategy is to draw on our own experiences to make these connections with our students. Reflect on your own teaching experience and write down three or four ways in which you commonly connect with students in your classes. You may choose to do this exercise with a colleague.

Then consider:

1. In making these connections would there be students who would feel excluded from these dialogues?
2. Are there situations where you feel uncomfortable in attempting to spontaneously interact and develop relationships with your students? What do you think contributes to this social discomfort?
3. Are there insights from this chapter about teaching diverse student groups that you can apply in your teaching *next week*? What are they and how will you use them in your specific teaching context?

CHAPTER 7

Assessment

Introduction

Many books have been written on the design and use of assessment to both promote and measure student learning. Our aim in this chapter is not to provide a 'how to' of assessment but rather to acknowledge the critical role of assessment in student learning, consider the changing landscape of assessment and examine tensions and challenges teachers and institutions experience around assessment.

Key aspects of assessment that need to be negotiated in the contemporary universities are, first, the tension between assessment for certification and assessment for learning and, second, the tension between assessing academic as opposed to workplace or everyday problems. Further, when we examine the teacher–learner relationship in the assessment process the capacity for conflict and negative emotions around assessment are evident. Teachers can be positioned in various ways in relation to assessment, from judge to guide to confidant. Support and clarity of expectations versus promoting student independence are just one area of possible anxiety. Where there is a mismatch between teacher and learner expectations of their relative positioning there is potential for tension and negative emotions. This can be heightened where students see themselves as clients not receiving the appropriate level of 'service' from their teachers.

There are tensions around the type of knowledge that will be assessed and the relevance of assessment to the contemporary workforce and society. Government and employers are emphasising the need for 'work-ready' graduates who can contribute to industry, the economy and society. Students are looking for assessment that is engaging and relevant to their personal experience. From educators there is a growing realisation that students need to learn not just for the current situation but to have the capacity for lifelong learning.

Our purpose in surfacing these issues is to help academics develop a critical understanding of their assessment practices and encourage assessment that provides learning experiences that engage students in the uncertainties, messiness and value conflicts of 'real world' problems. Before examining these issues in detail we set the scene with a discussion of why assessment matters and the changing nature of the assessment landscape in contemporary universities.

Why Assessment Matters

The centrality of assessment in student learning has long been argued. Boud (1988) emphasises that assessment methods and requirements probably have a greater influence on how and what students learn than any other single factor. Learners' understandings of what is legitimate and important can be significantly shaped by the assessment regime they experience. Further, as Boud reminds us, students can escape bad teaching but they can't avoid bad assessment.

If we accept that assessment frames learning and has more influence on learning than does teaching, it follows that assessment is a significant lever for change and improvement in students' learning experiences in higher education. In talking about changes to assessment practice Elton and Johnson (2002) draw attention to different degrees of change in assessment practice. These are improved practice with current assessment methods – *doing things better* and changes in assessment methods – *doing better things*. They assert that in the past decades educationalists have been much more concerned with new methods of assessment than improving current methods. They highlight that while both are important, small improvements in widely used assessment methods can have a greater over-all impact than innovative changes to assessment by a limited group of teachers.

If the importance of assessment is understood and the need for change acknowledged why don't we necessarily see a greater level of change occurring in assessment practice? Boud and Falchikov (2007) put forward a number of reasons both individual and institutional. First, it is a potentially risky and time-consuming business. Second, assessment has contributed to teachers gaining the positions they now hold so many have a considerable personal investment in what has appeared to work in the past. Third, assessment is a value-laden activity surrounded by debates around academic standards, measuring quality and graduate employ-ability. Deeply held positions about the nature and purpose of education underpin these debates. Despite these factors acting as barriers to change, there is gathering momentum for change in assessment practice in higher education, in part due to significant changes to the landscape of assessment.

The Changing Landscape of Assessment

We claimed in the introduction to this book that university work is located in a changing world and identified key features that lie at the heart of this change. Each of these features has an impact on assessment and contributes to creating a changing landscape of assessment. For instance:

- The growth of participation in higher education worldwide has resulted in rising student numbers, rising student–staff ratios and declining resources per student. This has created pressure for cost effective assessment.
- The increasing diversity of the student population has forced uni-versities to reassess accepted ideas about what can be expected from students and to provide greater support for students from diverse backgrounds to achieve assessment standards. Another fea-ture of the changing student body is competition from work and other commitments that engender a 'strategic' approach to study where assessed activities are often the only ones that are considered important.
- Demand from stakeholders that education be relevant to working life and for universities to produce 'work-ready' graduates has con-tributed to a focus on assessment of generic skills as well as disciplin-ary content and greater attention to 'authentic assessment'.
- Increased concern with accountability and quality assurance has seen greater institutional interest and intervention in assessment practice and standards.
- The transforming effect of information and communication techno-logies can be seen with new possibilities for assessment includ-ing online assessment with immediate feedback, asynchronous discussion-based activities and use of social networking tools such as blogs and wikis to give students greater control over assessment tasks. However, greater use of the Internet has also fuelled concerns about increasing incidence of plagiarism. (Plagiarism is discussed in Chapter 6.)

Tensions around the Multiple Purposes of Assessment

Assessment has multiple purposes in higher education and academics face a constant challenge in negotiating a balance between the tensions that these multiple purposes create. Traditionally assessment has provided a means of certification, identifying and discriminating between different levels of achievement, and between students (Bloxham & Boyd, 2007). This provides verification that a certain level of knowledge and skill has been demonstrated. In recent times, there has been increased scrutiny of certification from a variety of stakeholders including governments, accreditation agencies and/or peak bodies. A consequence has been rigorous accreditation provisions, audit mechanisms and requirements relating to standards and quality assurance processes. (These issues are discussed in detail in Chapter 2.) In this environment universities themselves have moved to intensify central regulation and control over the activities of departments and schools including assessment practices. From this perspective, where the purpose of assessment is certification, the focus is squarely on assessment *of* learning. Is the student's work deemed to have met the appropriate standard? Is this work comparable with standards on equivalent courses at other institutions?

However, if we view assessment from a student learning perspective our concerns will be much more directed to the role of assessment *for* learning and *as* learning (Bloxham & Boyd, 2007). More relevant questions will be: How does assessment engage students, shape their learning and provide experiences to extend and deepen their understanding? How does it contribute to their capacity to learn both currently and into the future?

Drawing attention to the current and future oriented functions of assessment Boud (2000) uses the term 'double duty' to reinforce the view that assessment needs to 'meet the needs of the present without compromising the ability of students to meet their own future learning needs' (p. 151) and position assessment as an indispensable accompaniment of lifelong learning. Assessment viewed in this way becomes important in developing students' evaluative and self-assessment skills in preparation for employment and a future of learning (Boud & Falchikov, 2007). This brings into question responsibility for assessment. Where assessment accompanies lifelong learning, learners will need to assume greater responsibility in the area of assessment and become capable self-assessors. This issue will be taken up in more detail later in this chapter.

The balancing of these seemingly divergent purposes of certification and fostering student learning through assessment is powerfully articulated by Light and Cox (2001):

For the student personally, and for the development of his or her sense of identity, the control and certification functions of assessment need to match the intellectual, personal, social and practical demands of a course. In this assessment needs to be less a rite of passage and more a significant and relevant personal achievement. This relevance needs to be apparent not just in terms of today's needs, reinforcing status quo, but in terms of the demands of tomorrow's 'super complex' challenges. Graduation must promise a stake in the future, not just the past; its rituals need to take students beyond traditional culture to a world of change and uncertainty. (p. 193)

Assessment cannot be considered in isolation of the complex social conditions in which it takes place. Of all aspects of teaching practice, assessment is the area where the power differential has the most potential to impact on students. Assessment is the basis on which qualifications are granted or withheld making it a primary location for power relations (Reynolds & Trehan, 2000). The emotionally laden context of assessment and the capacity for negative experiences around assessment to impact future learning experiences highlight the importance of a reflexive stance around assessment practice. In the following section we look more closely at teacher–learner interactions in the assessment process.

Teacher–Learner Interactions around Assessment

Much of what is written about assessment focuses on technical aspects with little consideration of the human dimension of assessment. Yet this does not align with our own experiences of assessment in our lives.

Assessing students is perhaps the most emotionally sensitive part of our education but at the same time is intellectually demanding and can be socially disturbing and divisive for students. It is easy for students to feel that it is not only their learning that is being assessed, but their developing identity as persons.

(Light & Cox, 2001, p. 169)

In Chapter 4 we examined teacher–learner relationships in a general sense. Here we consider relationships specifically around assessment and how assessment regimes shape teacher–learner relationships. With increasing focus being placed on student learning rather than teaching, and with learners being given more power and responsibility over what they learn, the 'teacher' can take up a number of positions. Teachers can be 'agents of certification', arbiters of what is worthy knowledge and whether students have performed to a satisfactory level. They can also be guides who help students develop their understanding in a discipline and learn from experience. Adding further to the complexity is the reality that students are not a homogenous body. Within any group of learners there exists a range of knowledge, expectations and dispositions. Carless (2006) speculates that it seems likely that better students are more receptive to feedback, because of their greater understanding of what good performance entails whereas for the weaker student feedback carries more risk of being discouraging and/or causing a misunderstanding.

Two significant and interrelated aspects of the teacher–learner relationship around assessment are worth examining in detail – the level of support and guidance given to students during and after assessment and communication with students about assessment. The way in which these are enacted can have a significant impact on student learning both at the time of assessment and into the future. Often discussions about quality of feedback focus on the technical structure of feedback such as its comprehensiveness and appropriateness. However, quality feedback is also about its accessibility to the learner as a communication, its catalytic and coaching value and its ability to inspire confidence and hope (Sadler, 1998).

For students who are anxious about assessment tasks frequent feedback can be beneficial. Yet there is a danger that students can become over dependent on support. An ongoing challenge for educators is balancing the provision of support with encouragement of independence. If we are too supportive of students and provide them with tasks that are highly structured we fail in both challenging them and encouraging the independence they need to build to engage with the complexity and 'messiness' of practice that they will encounter in their working lives. Yet where students see teachers as their guides they can become disappointed and angry at what they perceive as a lack of support. The process of receiving feedback and discussing it face to face can be challenging and become confrontational at times (Mutch, 2003).

Being aware of the emotional aspects of assessment can help teachers take a more reflexive approach, including developing strategies for diffusing potential conflict. One example would be introducing what is effectively a 24-hour 'cooling off' period between returning assignments to students and discussing their concerns with them. This can result in much more productive discussions as delaying consultations overnight can mean that the interactions take place in a less emotively charged environment. Students have generally recovered from their initial shock and disappointment and been able to reread their feedback in a calmer light and perhaps discussed their results with peers.

The issues raised in this section draw attention to two important aspects of assessment to which we will now turn in detail: communicating assessment feedback and helping students develop their capacity for self-assessment.

Communicating Assessment Feedback

To set the scene for this discussion of feedback it is important to briefly discuss different types of assessment. We have introduced earlier in this chapter the idea of the enduring tension between assessment for certification and assessment for student learning. This tension and the dual role of the teacher can be seen in formative and summative assessment. Formative assessment refers to assessment specifically intended to provide feedback to improve and accelerate learning (Sadler, 1998) whereas summative assessment is designed to sum up achievement and tends to come at the end of a learning sequence. The teacher's role as formative assessor is to engage with learners to facilitate development while their role as summative assessor is to stand back and provide judgement (Knight & Yorke, 2003). In practice the distinction between formative and summative is less pronounced than these definitions suggest. For example, some assessment items are specifically designed to fulfil a dual purpose. An assessment task submitted during a session of study can be formative because the student is expected to learn from the feedback provided yet still have a summative role because the grade awarded contributes to the overall grade for the unit of study (Yorke, 2003).

Formative assessment contributes to student learning through the provision of information, formally or informally, about performance. Yorke (2003) explains that this is underpinned by a triple intention: to give credit for what has been done to the expected standards, to correct what is wrong and to alert the students to possibilities they may not have previously discerned. Sadler (1998) identifies three elements typical of teacher feedback on assessment. First, the teacher considers the work that the learner has produced. Second, in what is invariably a comparative process, this is appraised against some background, or reference point. Sometimes this point of comparison is not explicit. Rather it is elusive, existing in some unarticulated or non-exemplified state inside the head of the assessor. Finally, to reflect their judgement, the teacher makes an explicit response such as assigning the learner's work a grade, a mark or a verbal statement about the quality itself including the reasons for the judgement and ways in which some of the shortcomings could be remedied.

The importance of formative assessment in student learning is well documented, in particular in an extensive study by Black and Wiliam (1998) across a wide range of educational settings. However, the complexity of the feedback process involved in formative assessment should not be underestimated. In recent years there has been a growing interest in moving beyond technical aspects of feedback (such as timeliness and comprehensiveness) to examining feedback as a process of communication. To a certain degree this research on communication around feedback has emerged from frustration by educators that many students don't appear to take heed of or act upon feedback given to them. This has led to the promotion of a more reflexive approach to interactions around feedback and greater acknowledgement of the impact of discourse, power and emotion on how messages are interpreted (Carless, 2006).

Higgins, Hartley and Skelton (2001) argue that communication 'works' because it is usually based on shared understandings and parties to the discussion having access to appropriate discourses enabling them to construct and reconstruct meaning from implicit messages. However, students often struggle to access the particular discourses underpinning feedback so Higgins et al. suggest that:

> Instead of asking if the student will take notice of feedback or whether it relates explicitly enough to the assessment criteria, or whether the quantity is sufficient, we should be asking how the tutor comes to construct the feedback, how the students understand the feedback (how they make sense of it), and how they make sense of assessment and the learning context in general. (p. 273)

In a similar vein Carless (2006, p. 231) cautions that 'assessment is too important for us to assume that students are on the same wavelength as we are'. Given the centrality of assessment to learning, he suggests lecturers need to engage with students in 'assessment dialogues' so students can learn about assessment in the same way that they engage with subject content. These 'assessment dialogues' can help students clarify 'the rules of the game', assumptions known to the lecturer but less transparent to the student. He identifies key areas where dialogue can be useful:

1. unpacking assessment criteria or involving students in generating or applying criteria,
2. clarifying that it is the assessment criteria that form the basis for the grade awarded and not other factors such as class attendance or performance, appearance, gender, ethnicity or hard work on the part of the student,
3. the marking process itself including the intention of written comments and how students might utilise these.

While feedback to students often focuses on the specifics of the particular task being assessed, Knight and Yorke (2003) argue that it is general feedback that has the greater power to stimulate student learning. This is linked to the notion of 'feedforward' where information is given about ways of improving performance on similar tasks in the future (Knight, 2007). Formative assessment can also play a significant role in helping students take greater control of their learning and become self-regulated learners. Central to self-regulation is the capacity to make sound judgements and this needs to be fostered in assessment regimes. For self- and peer-assessment to realise its potential students need to be:

> specifically inducted into the processes of making sound qualitative judgements, and defending them. In other words, the processes and resources that are accepted as natural and normal for the professional teacher need to be replicated for the students and built into their learning environment
>
> (Sadler, 1998, p. 82)

Key aspects of feedback practice that facilitate self-regulation are identified by Nicol and Macfarlane-Dick (2006, p. 205) based on a synthesis of the research literature on assessment. These provide a useful conclusion to this section on communication of feedback.

Good feedback practice:

1. helps clarify what good performance is (goals, criteria, expected standards);
2. facilitates the development of self-assessment (reflection) in learning;
3. delivers high quality information to students about their learning;
4. encourages teacher and peer dialogue around learning;
5. encourages positive motivational beliefs and self-esteem;
6. provides opportunities to close the gap between current and desired performance;
7. provides information to teachers that can be used to help shape teaching. (p. 205)

In the following section we will look at self-assessment and the role it can play in both current and future learning.

Developing Capacity for Self-Assessment

The capacity for self-assessment becomes a critical capability in a world of complexity and change. Boud (2000) argues that assessment should be seen as an indispensable accompaniment of lifelong learning and therefore must move from the exclusive domain of teachers into the hands of learners. Where students develop their own repertoire of assessment related practices they will be able to use these when confronted with learning challenges throughout their working lives (Boud & Falchikov, 2007). Yet while assessment is meeting future needs of students it must still perform the needs of institutions and students for certification.

Tan (2007) identifies three ways in which self-assessment practices are related to the development of students as lifelong learners. First, the development of critical skills that equip students to conduct and evaluate their own learning. This includes the ability of students to assess their progress and outcomes. Second, the fostering of self-directed learning where students are able to plan and direct their own learning in order to be able to pursue learning situations without the assistance of the teacher. Finally, accepting responsibility for learning in order to pursue responsibility for their learning beyond higher education.

Shifting sole responsibility for assessment from teachers intersects with debates around the type of knowledge that should be assessed and the relevance of assessment to the contemporary workforce and society. The idea of teacher-as-assessor assumes teachers have a mastery position over the domain of knowledge (Sadler, 1998). This is not generally the case in regard to workplace learning. Adult education discourses highlight a shift from viewing educational institutions as the principal sites of learning, to the recognition of the power and importance of workplace learning (Boud, 1998). Increasingly universities are exploring ways in which the workplace can be more effectively integrated into the university experience. (These are discussed in detail in Chapter 8 along with the pedagogical implications of this trend.)

'Authentic' assessment and workplace-based assessment enable closer links between student work and the type of activities that would be performed in the workplace. Workplace-based assessment addresses both the relevance concerns of students and recognises that they have a more complex identity than just that of a student. It allows them to draw on existing experience and capabilities but still have their worldview challenged and broadened. Further, it recognises the social practice of learning and effectively provides both an opportunity and a structure for students to situate their new learning in their local workplace. However, while authentic assessment is attractive as a concept it is not without its challenges and problems. These include whether tasks can really be considered 'authentic', and the complexity involved in making judgements in situations where students may demonstrate the desired learning in a way that is unspecified by the assessor. (Knight and Yorke, 2003, provide a detailed discussion on these issues.)

Students in this less structured learning environment will not be responding to clearly defined problems. They will need to develop the capacity to frame problems themselves to prepare for their assessment tasks but also as part of their journey into self-assessment and engagement in future professional life (Sadler, 1998). Moving assessment further into the workplace can also create challenges for academics. Academics are not necessarily experts in the specialised problems of individual workplaces, so their roles may be subtly or not so subtly changed. The position of academic shifts from a privileged position as disciplinary expert and knowledge disseminator to co-learner about workplaces, and provider of learning resources that will facilitate the student's capacity to generate their own knowledge in the workplace, currently and into the future. Increasing levels of self-assessment calls for a more reflexive engagement with assessment practice, both for academics and for students. This highlights the need for discussions of assessment practice to move beyond skills recognition to incorporate dimensions of the 'whole' person.

Shaping Worker Identities through Learning and Assessment

If identity work is seen as a reflexive process where learners engage in both self monitoring and monitoring of their relationships with others, self-assessment can be conceptualised as identity work. Contemporary individuals, Rose (1996) asserts, are incited to live as if making a project of themselves with a site within which individuals represent, construct and confirm their identity. The workplace is a key site for learning and identity work.

Timma (2007), reporting on study of workplace learning in three food production companies, comments that it is through the interconnected activities of work, learning and the performative assessment of skills that workers refine practices and construct meaning through their everyday embodied actions.

> The processes of thinking, acting and creating through the learning (and assessment), contribute to the formation of working and learning identities and it is this learning and knowing, as social participation, which has the capacity to profoundly connect identity and practice for workers. (pp. 165–166)

To further develop the idea of self-assessment as identity work we can bring together the dimensions of self identified by Timma (2005) in relation to assessment practice with the features Boud (2000) promotes in sustainable assessment. Four possible dimensions of self as identified by Timma (2005) are:

- Enquiring self – responsibility for assessment
- Expressive self – display skills and understanding
- Discerning self – learn to discriminate
- Accomplished self – self-worth at and beyond work

Sustainable assessment is a term used by Boud (2000) to highlight the need for assessment that develops the knowledge skills and dispositions to underpin lifelong learning. The following items are the basic resources he identifies as being necessary for sustainable assessment:

- Confidence that new assessment tasks can be mastered
- Exploration of criteria and standards which apply to any given learning task
- Active engagement with learning tasks with a view to testing understanding and application
- Development of devices for self-monitoring and judging progression towards goals
- Practice in discernment to identify critical aspects of problems and issues
- Access to learning peers and others with expertise to reflect on challenges and gain support for renewed efforts
- Use of feedback to influence new ways of engaging with the learning task
- Care in the use of language to avoid creating premature closure on ongoing learning.

(Boud, 2000, 161–162)

These items align readily with the different dimensions of self as can be seen in Table 7.1.

This analysis of dimension of self in relation to assessment in the workplace aims to progress understanding of how worker identities can be shaped by assessment and learning. While these discrete framings serve the purpose of analysis, they are, of course, interdependent.

Concluding Comments

Assessment practice is a critical area of teaching practice for beginning and experienced educators alike. Where academics are confronted with multiple demands and limited resources, the importance of assessment for student learning must never be forgotten. Even if we have to compromise on a number of desired teaching activities, good assessment practices should ensure good outcomes for our students. While acknowledging the certification role of assessment, we have argued the need for ongoing

Table 7.1 Workers as Lifelong Learners – Dimensions of Self in Relation to Assessment

ENQUIRING SELF	EXPRESSIVE SELF
Responsibility for assessment	**Display skills and understanding**
• Identify standards that should appropriately apply	• Overtly display skill and understanding
• Active engagement with learning tasks with a view to testing understanding and application of criteria and standards	• 'Show what you know'
	• Perform, explain, create
• Seek out learning peers and others with expertise to reflect on challenges and gain support for renewed efforts	• Create meaning from the assessment experience
• Use feedback to influence new ways of engaging with the learning task	• Convey essential meanings within the sociality of the workplace
DISCERNING SELF	**ACCOMPLISHED SELF**
Learn to discriminate	**Self-worth at work and beyond**
• Practice in discernment to identify critical aspects of problems and issues	• Confidence that learning tasks can be mastered
• Development of devices for self-monitoring and judging progression towards goals	• Mindfulness of language referring to own learning (to avoid negativity)
	• Care to avoid premature closure on ongoing learning

Source: Adapted from Boud, 2000 and Timma, 2005

attention to the role of assessment in building students' capacity to learn both currently and into the future. As we look to assessment as an accompaniment to lifelong learning our focus broadens from the technical aspects of assessment to a more holistic perspective where we can consider how learner and worker identities are shaped by assessment and learning and how we as educators are positioned by our assessment practices.

Enhancing Professional Practice

Review the assessment regime in a subject you are currently teaching and reflect on the following questions.

1. What does this assessment signal about what you see as being important in the subject? What messages are you sending to students through the assessment choices you have made and the priorities implicit in these choices?

2. Are there factors such as institutional directives or requirements from industry accrediting bodies that constrain your assessment practices? Can you design your assessment practices so that they meet these requirements while still providing the type of student learning experiences that you think are important in this subject? You may find it useful to discuss this issue with a colleague.

3. Is there potential in this subject to develop/further develop your students' capacity to self-assess?
4. Critically examine the range of assessment feedback employed in this subject. Do any aspects of it 'feedforward' into future student learning?
5. Have you ever experienced a very negative and emotional response to feedback you have given to a student? Think back to the circumstances of that event. Are there things that you would now do differently in that situation?

CHAPTER **8**

Promoting Workplace-Oriented Learning

Introduction

Education has always been concerned with identifying the kinds of skills and knowledge necessary for participating in productive work, family and social life. In recent times, however, there has been a growing demand from industry and government for universities to provide education that is more 'relevant' and pertinent to the needs of employers, which often means learning which is less abstract and discipline-bound and closer to the issues found in work contexts. This demand is seemingly driven by a concern with economic competitiveness in an increasingly globalised economy and with new views about what constitutes worthwhile knowledge.

We are told that the contemporary workforce needs to be highly skilled, adaptable and flexible. Such an 'adaptable, multiskilled and flexible work-force' implies one which can quickly and willingly apply existing knowledge and skills to new situations, and one which is prepared and capable of engaging in new learning as circumstances warrant. There are two related features of this new vision of the contemporary worker: one is the need to continually learn and update skills, presumably largely through experiences in the workplace; and the other is the need for a particular attitude or disposition towards work. Thus there is a dual expectation that universities will not only provide learners with work-ready knowledge and skill, but also with what may be called the 'soft skills': the dispositions, personal qualities and ways of being in the world that allow them to thrive and continue to learn (Barnett, 2006, p. 50).

With respect to 'work-ready' knowledge and skill, universities have explored ways in which the workplace can be more effectively integrated into the university experience. This typically occurs through professional placements in, say, architecture, cooperative education arrangements in business and engineering, clinical placements in medicine and nursing, practicum experience in teacher education and, in some instances, work-based learning awards where the work itself forms the basis of the curriculum. In addition, there is now a general acceptance of work-related projects and learning contracts as valid pedagogical tools. The workplace is thus increasingly present as a learning resource and a site of learning in the university sector. In many ways this is to be expected, given the growth in the demand for continuing professional education, and given the high number of mature age students in universities who insist on a curriculum and pedagogy which is relevant to their workplace experiences. This engagement with the workplace has led to a challenge to the traditional disciplines, partly because workplace problems are not neatly packaged into disciplinary areas, and partly because knowledge is increasingly seen as being 'produced' in the workplace. Indeed the idea of knowledge being produced in the academy and subsequently 'applied' to work, family and community life is no longer the sole way of depicting the relationship between the academy and the workplace.

With respect to the so-called 'soft skills', there has been a great deal of interest in identifying the employability skills developed at all levels and in all sectors of education. A consistent message from various reports into the skills needed is that while technical skills are recognised as important, by far the greater emphasis is placed on a range of generic skills such as communication, teamwork, problem solving, ongoing learning, creativity, cultural understanding, entrepreneurship and leadership. Universities have responded to this by attempting to specify what are generally called 'graduate attributes', 'generic skills' or 'employability skills'.

These two aspects of preparation for the world of work, work-related skills and knowledge and work-related personal dispositions, will be treated separately below.

As indicated above, although work-related learning can, of course, include a range of teaching strategies within universities, the main focus of this chapter is what universities can learn from current understandings of workplace learning: that is, how learning can be drawn from experiences in workplace settings.

The Workplace as a Site for Learning

Eraut (2004a) points to some crucial questions for those in universities concerned with either work placements or internships, or who draw upon students' workplace experiences for learning:

- What do we expect students to learn from experiences in workplace settings?
- How will learning take place?
- What factors will influence this type of learning?

There is a remarkable convergence in the responses to these questions in contemporary educational thinking. Kemmis (2005), for example, argues that 'professional practice knowledge':

> cannot be understood just from the perspective of knowledge 'in the heads' of individual practitioners . . . practice has a number of extra-individual features that need to be elucidated. These include such features as being formed and conducted in social settings, shaped by discourses, and being dramaturgical and practical in character. Taking these into account yields a richer view of practice, and makes it possible to understand more readily why changing practice is not just a matter for practitioners alone, but a task of changing such things as the discourses in which practices are constructed and the social relationships which constitute practice. (p. 391)

He analyses the kind of thinking – the practical reasoning – which is characteristic of the expert professional practitioner. Expert practitioners, he argues, are able to think reflexively and change their reading of a situation 'as it unfolds in and through practice' (p. 392). It is a mistake, he believes, to think about the workplace curriculum in terms of what needs to be 'in the heads' of students when they enter work settings.

> conceptualising what can be known in advance of practice captures only some of the features of the practices with which they are concerned. Harder to capture are the material, social, discursive and historical conditions and relations that shape and sometimes disfigure practice . . . to develop practitioners, practices, understandings of practice, and the changing settings of practice requires not only personal reflection in action, but also collaborative efforts by practitioners and those they serve to explore and grasp the complex and uncertain material, social, discursive and historical conditions of practice. (pp. 422–423)

Hager (2004) adopts a similar position when he critiques what he regards as the dominant view of learning as 'adding more substance' to the mind, which is a kind of container. This view of learning as a product is exemplified by:

> standard international educational nomenclature: acquisition of content, transfer of learning, delivery of courses, course providers, course offerings, course load, student load, etc. So despite advances in educational thought, the learning-as-product view has remained very resilient. It is as though formal education systems have never got beyond a mass production mindset reminiscent of the industrial era. (p. 6)

On Hager's account this learning-as-product mindset is based on two flawed assumptions, at least in so far as it applies to workplace learning. The first of these is that the products of learning are relatively stable over time, allowing knowledge to be incorporated into curriculum documents and textbooks and examined in standard achievement tests. The second assumption is that learning is replicable and comparable across learners, allowing us to make comparisons of their relative 'attainment'. Taken together, these assumptions support the view that practice is simply the application of theory: that there are general solutions to practical problems that can be developed outside of practice and that can be codified for application to the workplace. However, Hager argues that practice is much messier than this. For example, practitioners are not generally presented with 'ready-made' problems:

> problems are not presented ready-made, and [that], therefore, practitioners need to become proficient in problem-setting. Once a problem has been specified, it may not fit standard applied science categories. So both the data required and the solution method may be unclear. As well, the problem situation may be unique or unstable. This may require that the problem be continually redefined.
> (Beckett & Hager, 2002, p. 132)

Interestingly, this claim resonates perfectly with earlier work on practical intelligence in which Sternberg (1990) explores the different characteristics of typical intelligence test problems as opposed to the kinds of problems people encounter at work and in everyday life. They differ in six dimensions:

1. **Problem recognition and definition** – intelligence test problems typically define the problem and its parameters, while problem definition is much more open-ended in working life.
2. **Number of 'correct' answers** – intelligence tests typically have a

single correct or best answer. In working life the solution must be found among several possibilities.

3. **Access to complete information** – test problems typically include all the information necessary to solve the problem. By contrast, in working life all the information is rarely present and so there is a need to be able to act with limited, ambiguous or even conflicting information.

4. **Context** – problems on tests are typically decontextualised, whereas everyday problems are situated in a given context (why is the problem important? who has an interest in solving the problem? what events led up to the problem?).

5. **Feedback** – the feedback from test problems is usually quite unambiguous in that a score is allocated. By contrast, we rarely gain such unambiguous feedback from our performance on workplace problems, partly because of the continuing uncertainty of how successfully the problem was solved.

6. **Cooperative problem solving** – test problems are usually solved alone whereas work problems are typically solved in conjunction with others, or at least with the consideration of others' interests.

To return to Hager (2004), he goes on to support the emerging view of learning as a process. He draws on Dewey to make his point:

For Dewey, the overriding principle is that the good life for humans is one in which they live in harmony with their environment. But because the environment is in a state of continuous flux, so humans need to grow and readjust constantly to it so as to remain in harmony with it. Thus, for Dewey, education must instill the lifelong capacity to grow and to readjust constantly to the environment. Since, argued Dewey, reflective thinking as well as inquiry, democracy, problem solving, active learning, experiential learning, etc. are methods that are necessary for humans to learn to readjust effectively to the environment, these are the teaching/learning methods that must feature in education. Dewey argues that reflection is central to effective inquiry and problem solving, but this should not be seen merely in narrowly rational terms. For Dewey, reflective thinking is more holistic, incorporating social, moral and political aspects of the contexts in which it occurs. (p. 11)

This view of learning acknowledges the influence of historical, social and cultural factors and it points to the importance of dispositions and abilities, especially the ability to learn in new and changing environments.

This emphasis on historical, social and cultural factors has been taken up by others. The 'situated learning' approach of Billett advances the view that different forms of social practices lead to different ways of appropriating and structuring knowledge. His working out of this idea is quite elaborate, but basically he is saying that there are a variety of knowledge sources in a community of practice (such as other workers, hints, reminders, explanations, observations, listening, dealing with authentic problems, one's personal history), and that these have an impact on the way knowledge is appropriated and structured. He notes the constraints on the types of learning experiences available to workers, such as access to expensive equipment, employer and manager support for learning, the interests of co-workers in supporting other workers' learning and development, the influence of workplace affiliations and cliques and so on:

> In short, workplaces are contested learning environments in which relations among workers and support for learning are unlikely to be benign, because the learning and development of some workers may threaten others.
>
> (Billett, 2006, p. 41)

Lave and Wenger (1991) present a more radical view of 'situated learning'. For them, the essential thing about learning is that it involves participation in a community of practice: which is essentially a community engaged in a common set of tasks, with its associated stories, traditions and ways of working. At first this participation is peripheral (hence the term 'legitimate peripheral participation'), but it increases gradually in engagement and complexity until the learner becomes a full participant in the sociocultural practices of the community (an 'old timer' rather than a 'newcomer'). They point out the importance of having effective access to what is to be learned; and how the physical layout and the culture of work enhance or constrain participation by opening or closing opportunities for observation, mentoring, guidance and collaborative work. They emphasise access to practice as a resource for learning rather than instruction, and the value of relevant settings and strong goals for learning.

Their conception of learning entails quite a different mindset: away from the individual and towards the community. They are keen to distance themselves from the individualised psychological tradition which emphasises learning by doing, reflection on experience and a decentring from the teacher to the learner, emphasising the view that learning is an 'integral and inseparable aspect of social practice' (p. 31). Learning is not so much a matter of individuals acquiring mastery over knowledge and processes of reasoning, it is a matter of co-participants engaging in a community of practice. The focus is thus on the community rather than the individual. Allied to this view of the learner is a rejection of the idea that learners acquire structures or schemata through which they understand the world. It is participation frameworks that have structure, not the mental representations of individuals.

Three themes are present in much of the literature on workplace learning: the emphasis on the social and cultural nature of learning, the rejection of the 'mind as a container' metaphor and the attention given to the kinds of personal dispositions and qualities necessary to be an effective workplace learner. We now turn our attention to the last of these.

Work-Related Personal Dispositions

The 'soft skills' for work should really be thought of more holistically as the very dispositions and personal qualities which allow people to thrive in work, family and social settings. Views on the nature of these qualities and the role of the education sector in 'producing' these qualities can be found in various reports and inquiries sponsored by government at various levels, non-government organisations, industry peak bodies and intergovernmental agencies. A good recent international example is the set of final reports on the DeSeCo Project: a project set up by the OECD (2003) to draw on international best-thinking about what are 'key competencies for personal, social and economic well-being' in the 21st century. The report, *The definition and selection of key competencies*, identifies what competencies – apart from reading, writing and computing – are necessary for individuals to lead an overall successful life and for society to face the challenges of the present and the future. It named the three key areas for personal, social and economic well-being in the 21st century as: 'interacting in socially heterogeneous groups; acting autonomously; and using tools interactively'.

1. Interacting in socially heterogeneous groups

- Relate well to others
- Co-operate and work in teams
- Manage and resolve conflicts (p. 12)

These competencies are directed towards the capacity to function well in diverse groups and deal with 'differences and contradictions'.

2. Acting autonomously

- Act within the big picture or larger context
- Form and conduct life plans and personal projects
- Defend and assert rights, interests, limits and needs (p. 14)

The key competencies here:

> empower individuals to manage their lives in meaningful and responsible ways by exercising control over their living and working conditions. The ability to act within the big picture or the larger context; to form and conduct life plans and personal projects; and the ability to defend and assert one's rights, interests, limits, and needs are critical competencies for participating effectively in different spheres of life – in the workplace, in one's personal and family life, and in civil and political life.

3. Using tools interactively

- Language, symbols and texts
- Knowledge and information
- Technology (p. 10)

This is more than having the technical skills to use a tool (e.g. read a text, use a computer mouse) and includes an understanding of how the tool changes the way one can interact with the world and how the tool is used to accomplish broader goals.

The 'soft skills' that stand out and are repeated time and again in numerous government and intergovernmental agency reports worldwide are: teamwork, managing relationships, a capacity for innovation, enterprising skills, self-management, learning skills, flexibility, adaptability, creativity and a capacity for critical reflection on self, others and the broader context. An overarching competency is described in the DeSeCo Report as:

> Reflectivity – a critical stance and reflective practice – has been identified as the required competence level to meet the multifaceted demands of modern life in a responsible way . . . . an overall development of critical thinking and a reflective integrated practice based on formal and informal knowledge and experience of life. (p. 4)

What is the thinking behind these attributes? Where do they come from? First, it is clearly the business, industry and education sectors' reading of current economic circumstances and the skills needed in workplaces to compete in the global economy. Second, although perhaps less clearly, they represent a response to the broader circumstances of contemporary life – they are now seen as basic living skills.

In this context innovation, change and renewal are features of contemporary workplaces. Most changes imply a reorientation of persons' values or attitudes, the way they see themselves and their organisational knowledge (tacit, explicit and cultural). Recent interest by organisations, for example, in promoting 'cultural change' programmes for personnel suggests that business now regards the personal change of employees as crucial to the achievement of increased efficiency and profitability. The idea being that people who identify with the culture of an organisation are more likely to act in ways that contribute to the success of the organisation.

Specifically a new working self is demanded – workers are exhorted to be more flexible, multiskilled and self-reflective, with 'flexibility' including a willingness and capacity to take on new identities as they are demanded: such as when there is a corporate takeover or merger or a move from bureaucratic to more entrepreneurial activities, or where there are new technologies and work practices being introduced and so on. Thus in the name of 'learning for change' workers are invited, encouraged or otherwise cajoled into a great deal of 'self-work' (self-examination, self-reflection, self-monitoring, self-regulation). Included here are the increasing numbers of 'portfolio' workers, who do not have organisational allegiances but who are conscious of building their 'portfolio' of skills to maintain their position in the labour market.

In this context Barnett (2006) has observed that 'the fundamental educational problem of a changing world is neither one of knowledge nor of skills but is one of *being*. To put it more formally, the educational challenge of a world of uncertainty is ontological in its nature' (p. 51).

How can educators meet this challenge to equip students with the resources for self-formation and change – or if you like, for engineering and re-engineering themselves?

Arguably the changing nature of education and its interface with the workplace produces, presupposes or otherwise shapes new teacher/learner identities and pedagogical practices, and ultimately what it means to be a 'good' learner or teacher. For example, educators have long been concerned with developing the learning skills of students. This is a response to a commonly held view that teachers cannot be expected to teach 'everything', and therefore students need to be given the wherewithal to manage their own learning. It entails the development of a set of generic learning skills, but the skills typically identified are often only applicable to formal learning situations, such as listening, taking notes, summarising, questioning, finding information, organising and categorising thoughts, reviewing material for examinations, exam technique, learning how/when to generalise and how to apply theory to practice.

The shift to learning from experience in the workplace requires a reconceptualisation, or, perhaps more accurately, an additional set of skills and attitudes regarding learning, such as: how to analyse experiences, the ability to learn from others, the ability to act without all the facts being available, choosing among multiple courses of action, learning about organisational culture, using a wide range of resources and activities as learning opportunities (e.g. memos, policies, decision-making processes) and understanding the competing and varied interests in the shaping of one's work or professional identity. Learning from workplace experience also entails the identification and creation of opportunities for experiences from which new learning will flow. This may involve the learner/worker volunteering or seeking out special projects or assignments in the workplace, being active in suggesting initiatives in which he or she may be involved, negotiating with supervisors for more varied tasks and responsibilities or creating new ways of carrying out routine tasks.

At this point it should be clear that there is a convergence between work-related skills and knowledge and work-related personal dispositions. Some of the pedagogical implications of this are outlined in the next section.

Implications for Pedagogy

The pedagogical expertise of the educator takes on a new significance in the context of workplace learning: it shifts from being a content specialist towards helping learners develop the capacity to learn from their experiences. This is accompanied by the increasing importance and centrality of the 'learner' as opposed to the 'teacher' in the pedagogical process: learners are given more power and responsibility over what they learn and they are crucially seen as *producers* of knowledge. The 'teacher' in these circumstances can take up a number of positions: an arbiter of what constitutes worthy knowledge, a guide who assists learners to 'learn from experience', a measurement specialist who monitors performance, a facilitator who 'processes' the concerns and interests of learners, a commentator or decoder who addresses issues of power and authority or a manager of learning who ensures that the conditions conducive to learning are present in the workplace.

Following Eraut (2004a; 2004b) it is important to have a conception of the kinds of learning people engage in at work. To this end Eraut developed a typology to guide his research into workplace learning (see Table 8.1). He used it as a useful heuristic in his research but it can be equally applied to planning, recording and reviewing the kind of learning expected from work placements. It contains generic descriptors of tasks, skills, capabilities, knowledge and dispositions that can be developed in workplace settings (with the exception of the key skill of reflexivity, to which we will return).

With respect to the processes of workplace learning, Eraut (2004a) makes the point that workplace environments are only rarely structured with learning in mind and that the majority of learning in the workplace is informal – a combination of learning from other people and personal

Table 8.1 What is being Learned in the Workplace?

Task performance
Speed and fluency

Complexity of tasks and problems

Range of skills required

Communication with a wide range of people

Collaborative work

Awareness and understanding
Other people: colleagues, customers, managers, etc.

Contexts and situations

One's own organization

Problems and risks

Practices and strategic issues

Value issues

Personal development
Self-evaluation

Self management

Handling emotions

Building and sustaining relationships

Disposition to attend to other perspectives

Disposition to consult and work with others

Disposition to learn and improve one's practice

Accessing relevant knowledge and expertise

Ability to learn from experiences

Teamwork
Collaborative work

Facilitating social relations

Joint planning and problem solving

Ability to engage in and promote mutual learning

Role performance
Prioritization

Range of responsibility

Supporting other people's learning

Leadership

Accountability

Supervisory role

Delegation

Handling ethical issues

Coping with unexpected problems

Crisis management

Keeping up-to-date

Academic knowledge and skills
Use of evidence and argument

Accessing formal knowledge

Research-based practice

Theoretical thinking

Knowing what you might need to know

Using knowledge resources (human, paper-based, electronic)

Learning how to use relevant theory (in a range of practical situations)

Decision making and problem solving
When to seek expert help

Dealing with complexity

Group decision making

Problem analysis

Generating, formulating, and evaluating options

Managing the process within an appropriate timescale

Decision making under pressurized conditions

Judgement
Quality of performance, output and outcomes

Priorities

Value issues

Levels of risk

Source: Eraut, 2004b, in Rainbird, Fuller and Munro, 2004
Reproduced with permission from Taylor & Francis

experience. It is important, therefore, to identify the kinds of workplace activities which give rise to workplace learning. Eraut identifies four such activities which account for most of the learning: participation in group activities, working alongside others, tackling challenging tasks and working with clients. Other processes include formal training and the provision of resources such as manuals, reference books, etc., mentoring, supervision and coaching and informal support from peers. The kinds of learning activities embedded in these processes include formal study, listening, observing, reflecting, practising and refining skills, trial and error, problem solving, getting information and asking questions, developing a relationship with a wider network of knowledge resource people and giving and receiving feedback. Clearly, preparing students for work placements means ensuring they have an understanding of how learning occurs in the workplace and the actions they can take to enhance their learning.

Having explored the *content* and *process* of learning, Eraut (2004a) turns his attention to the factors affecting learning in the workplace.

> Our analysis suggests that a group climate for learning has to be created, sustained and re-created at regular intervals . . . this has to be a management responsibility . . . Hence, managers have to be educated and supported for this role. (p. 268)

He identifies three such factors associated with the *context* of learning and three factors associated with *learning and the learner.*

The context of learning

- The allocation and structuring of work
- Encounters and relationships with people at work
- The expectations of each person's role, performance and progress.

Learning and the learner

- The challenge and value of the work
- Feedback and support
- The confidence and commitment of the learner.

There are, of course, many ways of describing and analysing the factors affecting learning in the workplace context. Eraut (2004a) focuses on the structure of the work and how this structure affects opportunities for meeting and working alongside people, and whether the work is sufficiently challenging. Others such as Fuller and Unwin (2002), in a long-term research project in the UK, found that they could assign workplaces along a continuum from 'expansive' to 'restricted'. In 'expansive' workplaces, learning was valued and planned into the work process, the nature of the work required the use of a wide variety of knowledge and there was a culture of sharing knowledge and expertise. This was not the case in restrictive workplaces. After investigating learning in Norwegian companies, Skule and Reichborn (2002) identified seven factors that promote learning through work:

1. High degree of exposure to demands from customers, management, colleagues and owners.
2. High degree of exposure to changes in technology, organization and work methods.
3. Managerial responsibility.
4. A lot of external professional contact.
5. Good opportunity for feedback from work.
6. Support and encouragement for learning from management.
7. High probability that skills are rewarded through interesting tasks, better career possibilities or better pay. (p. 10)

Billett (2006) too has identified the factors that facilitate learning in the workplace, or 'affordances' as he calls them, such as the degree of routine, the degree of discretion, the range and complexity of activities and working with others. He is mindful of the pedagogical qualities needed:

These include assisting learners to understand the requirements for effective work: the curriculum goals. Like those stated in syllabuses, these goals may need to be made explicit and be the subject of intentional guided activities in the workplace, because what constitutes effective work-practice is often hidden or hard-to-learn ... Moreover, beyond the teachers' contributions are the kinds of opportunities, interactions, resources, and infrastructure that are available to provide appropriate learning experiences. Even with the best and most faithful intent, learners' experiences may be constrained by these factors, by the available curriculum. (pp. 37–39)

I cite these examples to illustrate how different researchers come to similar outcomes when describing the factors affecting learning at work. Of course, some of these factors are not relevant to work placements, and educators have a restricted capacity to influence the range of factors. But educators can use these factors to negotiate the nature of the experiences in which the students will be engaged, and they can provide some support for mentors or managers in the workplace.

With respect to the factors relating to the learner, Eraut (2004a) elaborates on the issue of the confidence and commitment of the learner:

The first thing that struck us in our interviews with novices and experienced workers in mid-career was the overwhelming importance of confidence. Much learning at work occurs through doing things and being proactive in seeking learning opportunities, and this requires confidence. Moreover we noted that confidence arose from successfully meeting challenges in one's work, while the confidence to take on such challenges depended on the extent to which learning felt supported in that endeavour. Thus there is a triangular relationship between challenge, support and confidence. (p. 269)

It is in this portrayal of confidence that Eraut comes closest to exploring the idea of *how to be* as a contemporary worker – but, unlike others (see Barnett, 2006; Rychen & Salganik, 2003; Kemmis, 2005), he stops short of engaging with this issue. This issue of *being* is arguably fundamental to the capacity to learn in new and changing environments, and to read a situation and change as circumstances warrant. Kemmis expresses this as follows:

wise practitioners stay open-eyed (to changing objective conditions) and open-minded (about changing subjective conditions): they set out to conduct their practice alert to whatever might become salient to their reading of themselves, their understandings and their situations, because these changing perspectives may – perhaps we should say 'almost certainly will' – cause them to change their views about the nature of their initially intended course of action and how things should unfold in this particular case. (p. 407)

The capacity for reflexivity is clearly the core skill underlying both the development of workplace knowledge and skill and the development of personal dispositions and ways of being in the workplace. By a 'reflexive engagement with the world' we mean understanding oneself and critically evaluating your 'self', the circumstances in which you live and the way you are positioned in all your relationships – in work, family, institutional and community life. From a pedagogical point of view this means providing learning experiences that engage students in the uncertainties, messiness and value conflicts of 'real world' problems. This is the great value of work experience and other work-focused learning activities such as portfolio development, reflective journals, work-based projects, action research, community-based projects and so on. The kinds of work-focused tasks that students now undertake provide the potential both for engagement with the world and for reflecting on and acting upon themselves.

To realise this potential students need to have the capacity to 'act upon themselves' in various ways. The typology below is arguably useful as a heuristic device for assisting students to extract this kind of learning from their workplace experience.

Knowing Oneself

This may take various forms such as examining one's world views, assumptions, and paradigms; bringing to conscious awareness previously repressed or hidden feelings and thoughts; analysing discrepancies between self-concept, self-esteem and ideal self; revisiting one's biography or life story; seeing oneself anew through the eyes of others or perhaps measuring oneself against established norms through undertaking psychological tests and completing psychological inventories. Typically, the exercise of knowing oneself is used to establish the groundwork for personal change. The literature is replete with techniques, processes and practices for knowing oneself, but the most visible and dominant is the examination of assumptions, paradigms and perspectives; that is, the examination and subsequent challenging of the lens through which you view the world.

Controlling Oneself (Self-Efficacy)

The work of self on self implies some degree of agency and control. Invariably, self-knowledge is not sufficient for reflexivity and the capacity for change. It is also necessary to act on those things that work against reflexivity: typically such things as everyday habits, patterns of interpersonal relationships, community and organisational structures in which one is embedded and broader social structures and agencies that oppress, deny or overly shape who you are. Many learning designs to promote reflexivity foster mastery and the exercise of authority over oneself; that is, self-regulation, self-monitoring and self-discipline, which may take forms such as personal goal setting, time management, daily planning or the practice of a daily regime of habits or exercises.

An important aspect of self-control is planning changes to the conditions in which you live and/or work and how they affect you. In the work context this may involve negotiating work redesign or new work tasks, challenging languaging practices that position you or others in unfavourable or demeaning ways and so on.

Caring for Oneself (Paying Attention to Oneself, Watch Yourself)

Many writers focus on the emotional, intuitive, extra-rational and intensely personal aspects of a reflexive engagement with the world (see Cranton, 2006; McWhinney & Markos, 2003). In such instances, learning designs incorporate elements such as confessional practices, cathartic experiences and the exploration of personal relationships at home and in the workplace. Practices used for this purpose may be writing letters to oneself, diary writing, the exploration of self-image and values, guided imagery, the documentation of critical life events or incidents, journalling, life history exploration and the exploration of one's own needs – emotional, intellectual, social and spiritual.

(Re)creating Oneself

A classic paradigm for learning designs that promote reflexivity is that of religious conversion: Confession is followed by renunciation and then by the affirmation of a new faith and the practices it entails. Arguably, many contemporary learning designs are secular versions of this road to Damascus – critical self-disclosure is followed by a form of renunciation (e.g. 'I renounce the way I have been the mouthpiece for an unethical organisation' or 'I renounce the way I have been narrated in the professional life') and then by a commitment to change. As always, the possibility of creating or recreating oneself raises questions about both the means and the ends of such an activity: is it about sustaining an 'authentic' you, asserting the autonomous 'you', becoming a more conscious 'being in the world', telling new stories about your 'self' or consciously constructing new patterns of interpersonal relationships? In addition, the relationship between the 'new' and 'old' you is also important – is the old you 'discarded' as being irrelevant to the new you, or is it reinterpreted to provide a sense of coherence and continuity with the past?

Of course the different pedagogical designs that invite students to act upon themselves in various ways do not guarantee that students will develop the capacity for 'reflexive engagement' as we have described it. Promoting a 'critical' engagement is the key – which allows the possibility of overturning existing practices rather than simply aligning oneself with institutional priorities, goals, visions and ways of doing things. Loyalty, a prized personal attribute of business, is certainly a secondary quality to a critical questioning mind, and this is perhaps where the interests of educational institutions and the interests of employers part company.

Summary

This chapter commenced with the observation that universities are under pressure from governments and industry groups to produce more work-ready graduates. Contemporaneously, the knowledge economy is repositioning what we mean by knowledge and is challenging the traditional conception of universities as the producers of knowledge, which is then 'applied' to the workplace. The proposition is that significant knowledge is produced in the workplace itself. Universities have responded by attempting to include more workplace related learning in the curriculum, but by and large this has not been informed by an understanding of the workplace learning literature. In exploring workplace learning this literature highlights the different kinds of skills and knowledge gained from workplace settings, and points to a need to think differently about learning, especially the idea that learning is not simply 'in the heads' of individual learners, but involves consideration of how learning is formed in social settings and shaped by discourses within the workplace. This led to an examination of the organisational and individual factors that promote learning in the workplace. An important individual disposition is the capacity for adaptation and change in response to changing circumstances. Such a disposition is premised on our ability to reflexively engage with workplace problems and issues, which involves critically reflecting on oneself and a learner and worker. Finally, we have highlighted some pedagogical strategies which can assist learners to gain the knowledge skills and dispositions required for effective engagement with the workplace.

Enhancing Professional Practice

Exercise 1

Prepare a one page set of guidelines (in point form) for students who are about to undertake a work placement. The guidelines should alert them to the possibilities of learning, the observations they can make, the interactions they can seek out and the documentation they would need to provide to show that they were reflexive learners.

Exercise 2

Using the material in this chapter prepare a list of focus group questions aimed at drawing out the learning experiences of students who have recently completed a work placement. Compare your list with colleagues; discuss and amend your list as needed.

CHAPTER 9

Learning in the Digital Age

It is commonplace for educators to remark that good-quality teaching and learning should not be driven by advances in technology, that we should not adopt the latest technology for the sake of it and that we should appraise each new development in terms of how it adds value to our current conceptions of educational worth. That is, technology is there to serve the interests of education – it is simply a tool like any other that should be used in the service of educational ends. On this account what constitutes 'good education' appears to be independent of technology and its broader social impact. An opposing view is that the social impact of advances in technology has fundamentally changed the way in which we interact with others and the broader world – so much so that the students of today, whom Ashraf (2008) has called the 'Google-eyed YouTube generation', are no longer the people our educational system was designed to teach.

No amount of hyperbole can capture the breathtaking advances in technology since the advent of the Internet (for a good summary see Downes, 2008). It is a story of increasing bandwidth so that the sharing of text, images and video is now a mainstream activity. Wireless technologies have allowed more mobile Internet connections, the processing power of computers has increased from megabytes to gigabytes, there is a growing capacity to store information, the software systems are more reliable, personal and user-friendly and digital technology is becoming part of our everyday lives. As of 30 June 2008 world Internet usage has increased to 21.9% of the total world population. This represents a 305.5% surge in usage growth in the past eight years alone (Miniwatts Marketing Group,

2008). Market research in the US shows that 'consumers age 18 to 27 say they use the Internet nearly 13 hours a week, compared to 10 hours of TV' (Byron, 2008). Downes (2008) presages the educational possibilities quite nicely:

> The combination of portable and affordable computing devices, combined with widely available digital presentation tools, will make education genuinely personal and portable.
>
> Imagine having in your hands a device on which you can not only write or type content, but which takes photos and records videos. Imagine further that this device contains easy-to-use but powerful photo and video editing software, and is additionally connected to a massive library of content made available through ambient broadband internet connections.
>
> Moreover, imagine that any environment that contains a flat surface can become a teaching environment, one where your friends' faces (or your parents' or your teachers') can appear life-size on any old wall or on a table surface as you converse with them from the next room or around the world. (p. 9)

The promise of digital technology for education has always been the liberation of time and place, so that students could study at a time and place of their choosing. In the early years this was translated into a more effective means of delivering distance education, supplemented by electronic communications through email. What could not be anticipated was the growth in the ability to communicate through blogs and social networking sites such as MySpace and Facebook, the ability to access information and resources through the Internet, the ability to produce content through readily available presentation software and the capacity to do all this in a way which was mobile, personal and global. How all this may impact the future shape of education will be taken up towards the end of the chapter, but first we should note that by and large educational institutions have thus far managed to preserve their world: one where the essential features of the face-to-face classroom have been incorporated into online learning. We see this in Web CT and Blackboard and even in Second Life where the essential thrust has been to mimic the classroom – it is the translation of the classroom into a digital environment. Even this rather constrained take-up of digital technology has produced quite a revolution in education with accompanying changes in teachers' skill sets, in the working environment of teachers and in the way teachers and students communicate.

Before exploring some of these changes we should note that the online delivery of courses has rapidly become the fastest growing segment of higher education. In the US, for example, approximately 20% of all students enrolled in higher education are taking individual courses online. This growth is considerably higher for older students, over the age of 25, who are increasingly taking their entire higher education programme online (Arbogast, 2008). Online usage figures often capture only one small segment of the e-Learning picture. Interpretation of usage data is more complete when consideration is given to enhanced, hybrid and blended course delivery in addition to the 100% online format. When all forms of e-Learning are combined we have even more dramatic increases. Results from the American Association of Community Colleges Instructional Technology Council annual national member survey documents robust growth of 17% to 18% in distance education for each of the past three years. This growth rate is particularly dramatic when compared to overall campus enrolments which average only a 2% growth rate (Lokken, Womer & Mullins, 2008). In 2007 online enrolments at universities in the US experienced a 12% annual increase. With this growth come changes to the higher education market of student recruitment. Close to 70% of higher education institutions are now reporting growing competition for online students (Allen & Seaman, 2008).

We can draw several particularly interesting e-Learning trends from this discussion.

- Older students, over the age of 25, have become the early majority participants.
- Growth is impacting all levels of higher education including community college, university undergraduate and, particularly, graduate programmes.
- Competition is heating up among higher education institutions as online delivery dissolves the artificial boundaries established to serve students in the conventional face-to-face format. With no boundaries, the university service area is now part of a competitive global market.
- Academics are expected to assume the responsibility to meet these growing demands of information and communication technologies (ICT) upon instructional delivery.

Changes in Teaching Skills

Competence in online instruction encompasses many skills that are likely to be new to educators. Typically we approach the challenge as if we are teaching a face-to-face course – or at least we use our face-to-face experience as the default position for online learning. The following table segments elements of instructional practice into three columns representing the tensions we experience as we design and implement online learning.

Table 9.1 Online Teaching and Face-to-face Teaching

Online Teaching		Face-to-face Teaching
Technological skills	**Online content delivery**	**Conventional classroom**
Knowledge of Language Management System platform (e.g. Blackboard, Desire2Learn, Moodle)	Define virtual presence and private space of the teacher	Lesson plans
Basic computer skills with hardware and software	Course material posted in a standardised format	Scaffold material delivery with immediate student feedback
Online Internet access	Download	Enter the classroom
File management (e.g. pdf, htm, txt, rtf, doc, docx, jpg, gif)	Select and post content links	Photocopy handouts Overhead transparencies
Basic troubleshooting technical support for students	Threaded discussions	Class discussion
Interface with IT department	Help desk	Teacher managed

The table demonstrates how our application of technological skills and online content decisions are often blurred during the instructional design process. It is interesting to note that when we consider our teaching practices in the conventional classroom in comparison to an online delivery, the steps are more distinct. Also of interest is the number of activities in online teaching that require the teacher to work with others and relinquish control of instructional delivery.

When teaching online we cannot simply transfer the conventional lesson plans we use in the classroom to the online learning environment, since students interact with material differently when online and face-to-face. Often we find that activities that work in the classroom typically cannot directly transfer to online, nor do online activities conveniently adapt to conventional classroom delivery. For example, an important consideration is the way in which the group dynamics of online learning groups differ from those of face-to-face-groups. In a review of this issue, Hron and Friedrich (2003) identify the specific characteristics of net-based collaborative learning. For them some of the more notable characteristics (taking text-based asynchronous learning groups as the norm) are the following:

- Absence of non-verbal cues
- Normal rules for social interaction (e.g. turn-taking) are suspended

- There are temporal delays in communication
- There are additional demands on learners (e.g. learning to operate complex technology) and the effort required to actively participate.

Hron and Friedrich argue that these features produce a range of difficulties for learning groups, such as difficulties in maintaining topic coherence and difficulties in understanding the context of a message. It is difficulties such as these that drive the efforts of instructional designers and online moderators in the development of new online collaborative learning methods:

> These methods structure the interaction and learning processes of the group members and seem therefore to be apt to cope with problems of net-based message exchange and participation. Collaborative learning methods range from global learning methods for organising group work to behaviour rules for structuring dialogues, so called co-operation scripts . . . aimed at controlling the dialogue of the group members. (p. 73)

It is clear that online learning groups are, in themselves, very different from face-to-face groups and that their group dynamics differ – or at least that the way in which group phenomena are played out is different. Furthermore the various attempts of instructional designers or group moderators to overcome the difficulties and challenges of online learning have a direct effect on the dynamics of the group. While this is also true for face-to-face learning groups, there is a tendency (which is quite counter-intuitive) to have more highly structured interactions in online learning, and there is a reduced possibility of responding to learners' feedback to change the structure. Jaques and Salmon (2007) argue that most of the usual behaviours of groups are evident in online learning but they emphasise that 'it is even more important in virtual groups to make members aware of ways of achieving successful team formation and allocation of roles and responsibilities, since these are unlikely to merely emerge' (p. 160). Arguably the take-up of online learning has led to more formal delivery of content and more structured interactions among participants rather than the kind of free-flowing and spontaneous communication evident in social networking sites. This is well illustrated in Hron and Friedrich's (2003) depiction of the skills and functions of the online moderator as shown in Table 9.2.

As Hron and Friedrich point out, many of the rituals and procedures in face-to-face groups need to be made more explicit in the online environment. This results in a highly structured set of actions on behalf of the teacher and tasks on behalf of the participants. Not only do teachers need to develop a set of new skills but there are a host of skills that learners need to develop to participate fully in online learning. Clarke (2008) describes a

Table 9.2 Moderation Functions and Measures

Organisation function	Motivation function	Expert function	Didactic function
Give an overview about the course, make relations between instructional media (print, computer based training) and learning forms (group and individual work).	Support social presence e.g. by introduction of turns.	Supervise suitability of contents and materials regarding curricular goals.	Give introducing hints/processing assistance for topics.
Specify goals for course episodes.	Create discussion-favourable climate e.g. by welcome messages and encouragement.	Affect topics according to curricular goals.	Stimulate summing up of complex topics or give summaries.
Support formation of groups.	Give feedback e.g. react immediately to each first contribution.	Enter additional contents and materials.	Ask comprehension questions.
Open and terminate course episodes.	Induce commitment, specify communicative minimum requirements, introduce netiquette.	Establish subject matter relationships between topics and learning groups.	Subdivide a range of topics into sub-tasks, which can be cooperatively worked on.
Plan meta communication e.g. evaluation of the course by the learners themselves.	Stimulate curiosity and cognitive conflict e.g. raise questions, present contradictory positions.	Make sure that materials are suitably used.	
Inform about performance and grading.			

Source: Hron and Friedrich, 2003
Reproduced with permission from Wiley-Blackwell

range of information communication and technology skills that are needed, such as understanding the options available in the operating system to make the system more accessible, file management, file formatting, compressing files, tracking changes, saving and backing up information, searching the World Wide Web, presenting information such as tables, charts and graphs, creating and importing images and sound files, blogging, downloading podcasts, using utilities effectively and so on. It should also be noted that technology has its downside – users typically need help and Internet connections are not always reliable. The Pew Internet and American Life Project reports that 48% of technology users usually need help with the set up and functioning of new devices. When we consider that 44% report that their home Internet connection has failed in the past year it becomes fairly clear that our online students experience ongoing frustration with technology related issues when engaged in online learning (Horrigan, 2008). Imagine teaching in a conventional classroom as the lights are randomly turned on and off throughout the class session. What impact would this have upon you and upon your students? As teachers, we must factor into our planning of online delivery an awareness that neither we nor our students will experience a seamless interaction with online course delivery. It is essential that we develop and implement strategies to address our resulting frustration and respond to the learning stress students experience as we more heavily adopt the use of ICT.

Changes in Teacher and Learner Communication

It is interesting to consider the changes in teacher and learner relationships that are being adopted due to the growing role of e-Learning. A prominent shift that is commonly experienced by teachers involves changes in our communication with students. One of the more interesting phenomena a teacher experiences when working with students in an online environment is the ubiquitous influence technology has upon the teacher–learner relationship. As professionals we have grown accustomed to the sensation of being connected. Our professional community can be instantly accessed. Communication, knowledge retrieval and our identity are now digitally shaped and defined. Our students are also experiencing the subtle influences of technology upon daily life. As a result, both teacher and student exist in a state of feeling digitally connected everywhere at once. The time-honoured relationships between teacher and student are changing. An assumption students more frequently carry into their digital relationship with their teacher is 24/7 access. Academics now struggle with controlling the impact technology is having upon the work day and upon personal time. As reported in a recent review, 'Technology has made academics hyperaccessible. Many feel they now have to be hyperresponsive' (Fogg, 2008). Using the tools of technology wisely is essential to controlling excessive student time demands.

One method of controlling excessive teacher–learner communication is the adoption of asynchronous communication in e-Learning. The student may access instructional materials around their personal and professional schedules. Threaded discussion forums and postings are date and time stamped and accessed at the choosing of the student. Control over the learning environment provides a strong enhancement to many learning styles. This environment can carry over to the student's expectations regarding access to the instructor. An instructor can structure student access through formal announcements and postings of guidelines. The benefits of asynchronous communication break down quickly, however, when the teacher–learner relationship adopts more individualised informal online exchanges. In response, teachers find they must establish new standards of conduct and structured rules for student interaction (such as those proposed above by Hron and Friedrich, 2003).

For clarification let us consider a scenario. A teacher receives an unsigned email from svg1. The teacher assumes the message is from a student because the content of the message relates to a topic recently discussed in a student seminar at the university. How should the teacher respond? Does the teacher ignore the message? Not likely. The teacher may attempt to identify the sender by reviewing their folders for prior emails, checking electronic student lists or using the university internal people search engine function. Perhaps the teacher quickly replies to the message inquiring the identity of the sender. Does this imply the teacher is disconnected from the students? What are the implications for the student? Is this a simple breakdown in communication etiquette or does this imply the student assumes a more personal connection with the teacher? Given the complex power dynamics between teacher and student such simple actions are open to interpretation by either party and may create unanticipated results. This scenario raises larger issues regarding the identity and connection of the student with the teacher and with the institution of higher education. Communication through technology has created an environment whereby we must rethink our roles and responsibilities as teachers.

Communication challenges with students can also be found within a key feature of online delivery. The online discussion board feature stands out as an ongoing challenge for teachers to effectively adapt. Death by discussion board is quickly rising to the same level of notoriety as death by PowerPoint. This criticism of the discussion board occurs when a good tool is incorrectly designed and excessively applied. The result is that students quickly disregard the discussion board as an impediment to their learning. To avoid this critical mistake creative options and instructional strategies need to be identified and integrated into the design of an online course. Drawing a clear distinction between pedagogical practices and the processes of the tool is an essential first step to designing effective online instructional delivery. In so doing, our design approach recognises that online teaching is different from conventional classroom teaching. A five-stage model of teaching and learning online developed by Gilly Salmon (2003) is useful for understanding the pedagogical factors that shape this unique learning environment.

Individual access and the ability of participants to use online [technology] are essential prerequisites for conference participation. Stage two involves individual participants establishing their online identities and then finding others with whom to interact. At stage three, participants give information relevant to the course to each other . . . At stage four, course-related group discussions occur and the interaction becomes more collaborative . . . At stage five, participants look for more benefits from the system to help them achieve personal goals, explore how to integrate online into other forms of learning and reflect on the learning processes. (pp. 28–30)

The online engagement of the student with others at each of these learning stages clearly involves much more than interacting with the computer. One aspect of this complexity can be drawn between the virtual online experience and the conventional classroom. In the classroom the learning environment is physically defined and the teacher has immediate synchronous interaction with all students. A virtual learning space, however, represents a blurring of public and private space for the students and the teacher. The sharp distinctions and personal boundaries evident in the physical world are defined differently online (Beddows, 2008). Our role as teachers is to recognise this complexity and be sensitive to the unique demands that the online learning environment places upon each student. The sensitivity to the learning needs of our students will be defined and governed by our online communication and subsequently shape their learning experiences.

Changes in Work Practices

As mentioned above, teachers are more than ever required to work with others in the delivery of content and the design of learning. That is, educational work has become more distributed in the organisation. This means that teaching moves from a private space where teachers have more degrees of freedom, to a public space where the educational content is crystallised well in advance of its delivery according to a schedule determined by the requirements of the technology. For example, something as simple as a welcome to students and an outline of the course, which may be almost improvised or prepared on the day of delivery in a face-to-face class, needs to be prepared well in advance in an online environment. The welcome may also be integrated with a broader welcome to the university posted by the Dean or Provost, and you will need to take care that your welcome 'text' is consistent with this broader message. In preparing this text some questions may come to mind such as 'Does your welcome express the vision and purpose of the university?', 'Does it fit well with the statement of graduate attributes?', 'Is it sufficiently encouraging of minority groups, and does it use inclusive language?' In an online environment, where the text is very public and open to scrutiny and less nuanced by non-verbal cues, these considerations take on a new significance. They have the effect of firmly embedding teachers in the culture and practices of the institution.

Additionally, as demands upon our time shift to online tasks teachers find themselves increasingly working at a computer. The work location is now determined primarily by computer access. Where we are geographically is no longer relevant to defining our classroom as long as our students are provided with a sense of assurance that they are connected to us. Yet, we find ourselves increasingly pulled to physically participate and connect to our campus community. Given this paradigm shift in work setting it is ironic that the traditional expectations of the workstation remain relatively unchanged. This is not to argue against academic collegiality or campus service. Rather, we are grappling with a social tendency to fill the void of conventional teaching with ancillary duties and activities. The increasingly dated notion of maintaining office hours is one particularly vexing example of this demand pulling upon our professional time. In response we often attempt to address all competing productivity expectations and give more of our time and energy than is feasible or healthy. Unfortunately, academic workload at public higher education institutions in the US and elsewhere has seen a continued overall increase. This workload increase includes a greater number of classes taught, publications in referred articles, professional contributions and the management of research projects (Townsend & Rosser, 2007). Meyer (2008) provides a valuable perspective to the issue of faculty workload and the misconceptions of unlimited online capacity. 'Capacity may be less dependent on faculty time, but only if the online course is competently redesigned' (p. 63). Somewhat ironically the promise of technology to liberate us from time and place has not been accompanied by a lessening of the demands placed upon us – quite the contrary, a 24/7 world for the students is translated into something approximating a 24/7 life for teachers in higher education. The term 'blended learning' can be extended to include the concept of 'enmeshed learning' – the way in which learning (and teaching) has become 'enmeshed' into our everyday lives, so that our MP3 players and mobile phones become sites of work and learning as we shift seamlessly between recreation, education and entertainment.

Downes (2008) sees contemporary information and communication technologies as ultimately deschooling society. He notes that online learning has hitherto been constrained by entrenched educational and institutional conventions such as the class or cohort as the unit of learning, with a group of people starting at the same time, proceeding roughly at the same pace, engaging in the same assessment, being graded and ending at the same time. He advocates a break from this convention so that students can set their own curriculum and proceed at their own pace. He sees the role of educational institutions as being to foster participation in learning networks.

> The purpose of educational institutions, therefore, is not merely to create and distribute learning opportunities and resources, but also to facilitate a student's participation in a learning environment – a game, a community, a profession – through the provision of the materials that will assist him or her to, in a sense, see the world in the same way as an accomplished expert; and this is accomplished not merely by presenting learning materials to the learner, but by facilitating the engagement of the learner in conversations with members of that community of experts. (p. 23)

And later:

> In the end, what will be evaluated is a complex portfolio of a student's online activities (Syverson & Slatin, 2006). These will include not only the results from games and other competitions with other people and with simulators, but also their creative work, their multimedia projects, their interactions with other people in ongoing or ad hoc projects, and the myriad details we consider when we consider whether or not a person is well educated. (p. 26)

Ultimately he sees learning as being thoroughly situated in 'real life' environments, with students making a real contribution to the business or enterprise in which they are located. This of course resonates quite well with the idea of the 'worker-learner' as explored in Chapter 8.

Downes' rather dazzling prognostications for the future of education will no doubt be realised in part. Mainstream journals are currently exploring the new Web 2.0 services and how they allow for greater interactivity, learner choice, autonomy and networking opportunities for creating and sharing knowledge. McLoughlin and Lee (2007) outline the dimensions of what they term Pedagogy 2.0:

- Content: Micro units of content that augment thinking and cognition; learner-generated content that accrues from students creating, sharing and revising ideas;
- Curriculum: Not fixed but dynamic, open to negotiation and learner input, consisting of 'bite-sized' modules, interdisciplinary in focus and blending formal and informal learning;

- Communication: Open, peer-to-peer and multi-faceted, using multiple media types to achieve relevance and clarity;
- Process: Situated, reflective, integrated thinking processes; iterative, dynamic and inquiry-based;
- Resources: Multiple informal and formal sources that are media rich and global in reach;
- Scaffolds: Support for students comes from a network of peers, teachers, experts and communities;
- Learning tasks: Authentic, personalised, learner-driven and designed, experiential and enabling multiple perspectives. (p. 669)

McLoughlin and Lee go on to provide examples of the above dimensions in practice, such as the distribution of *iPod Photo* players to Education freshmen in order to record study group sessions and to maintain audio blogs to connect with peers during work experience (Drexel University, US); students taking charge of producing talkback radio style podcasts (Charles Sturt University, Australia); peer teaching using podcasts (Bentley College, US); the creation of a wiki-based encyclopaedia by students covering ideas in law and criminal justice (University of North Carolina, US); the sharing and coordination of knowledge through blog posts and bookmarks with keywords or tags (University of Michigan, US); students preparing their own work to contribute to a professor's bilingual podcast feed and blog aimed at those studying Japanese as a foreign language (Osaka Jogakuin College, Japan); and the use of blogs, wikis and podcasts for virtual collaborative clinical practice in health education (University of Plymouth, UK).

In addition to the cumulative effect of small experiments and innovations such as those cited above, education will also change as the demands and expectations of the Google-eyed YouTube generation become more insistent. But it is not technology per se that will drive this – it will be the indirect influence of technology on how we conceptualise worthwhile knowledge. The debate concerning the nature of worthwhile knowledge is, of course, a continuing one with a long history, one that will continue to be shaped by social and technological change and by the shifting interests of industry, commerce, the professions and government.

Enhancing Professional Practice

Exercise 1 – Improving Strengths

This exercise is designed as an aid to stimulate self-reflection. By taking a quick snapshot of your online delivery practices you become more aware of your areas of strength as an online teacher. The premise behind this exercise is that you need to more aggressively pursue what works and in so doing rapidly adopt formative improvements in delivery. Thus, you are positioned to enhance your enjoyment of teaching.

1. List two things you enjoy about online teaching.
2. List two things you feel you do well as an online teacher.
3. Identify the common elements of practice among the four items on your list. What are you doing that is the same in all four items?
4. Brainstorm strategies to more effectively integrate these common elements into your online course. Share your ideas with colleagues and/or your university professional development teaching centre to promote further refinement.

For a more formal self-assessment tool please refer to the article, 'Using radar charts with qualitative evaluation: techniques to assess change in blended learning'. The article provides a framework using radar charts adapted from the field of organisational development. A modified six-zone radar chart comprised of six related variables (dynamics, assessment, communication, independence, richness and content) is used to assess the extent of blended learning in order to compare changes in the learning environment (Kaczynski, Wood & Harding, 2008).

Exercise 2 – Journey of Structured Experiences

This exercise is designed to document over time your online teaching journey and the learning journey of your students. Writing personal journals requires considerable self-discipline and is often lost among our other daily demands. A method to promote writing can be drawn from qualitative research. This practice involves writing memos addressing three different stages of a journey; reflective memos about the researcher as instrument, design memos about flexible emergent design considerations and analytic memos about the inductive/deductive shifts that occur during interpretation and analysis of data. The following steps are based on these techniques.

1. Assign your online students to write a short memo that identifies a learning objective from the course content that they found to be difficult or challenging to grasp.
2. Next, summarise a list of the challenging learning objectives and post it online. Assign students to pick one of the challenging learning objectives and propose an instructional strategy to more effectively deliver online.

3. Incorporate, as appropriate, student strategies into your online course.

You may want to maintain a record of the student memos and student strategies for future reference as you continue to reflect on and improve your online instructional course delivery practices.

CHAPTER 10

Postgraduate Research Education

Introduction

Students embarking on doctoral study have available to them a wide range of books offering advice on how to complete the various stages and phases of their dissertation and how to engage productively with their supervisors and mentors. Typical titles available include *How to complete and survive a doctoral dissertation* (Sternberg, 1981), *How to get a PhD* (Phillips & Pugh, 2000), *Authoring a PhD* (Dunleavey, 2003), *The unwritten rules of PhD research* (Rugg & Petre, 2004) and *Getting a PhD* (Finn, 2005). That commercial publishers have identified a market for such books is testimony to the growing numbers of aspiring doctoral candidates. But it signals more than that, perhaps the academy is not paying enough attention to the broad range of practices that make up a typical doctoral candidature, or perhaps the process of undertaking a doctorate is inherently amorphous. Probably both are true, partly because doctoral education has not been (until recently) the subject of educational debate and theory at the level of method, curriculum, teacher–learner relationships, and the learning environment, and partly because its status as 'education' is unclear.

A unique aspect of doctoral education is that it occupies a hybrid space between 'teaching', 'learning' and 'research'. The supervisory relationship foregrounds an ongoing tension in professional academic life; the tension between identifying as a 'teacher' on the one hand and a 'researcher' on the other. Research students are partly research colleagues and partly students, making the position of the supervisor ambiguous – as *researchers* the students should exhibit autonomy, independence of thought and originality; as *students* they are dependent on guidance and feedback and need to be prepared to take direction. Playing out this dual role is complex and demanding. It is no wonder that doctoral education has the potential to be highly emotionally charged, especially when the student's investment in time, energy and money is added to the mix.

It is also an area that is peculiarly subjected to institutional control, with most universities, and national bodies, adopting codes of practice that specify the respective institutional and individual responsibilities in doctoral candidature – such as frequency of meetings, the provision of timely feedback, the need to negotiate intellectual property and publishing arrangements, the provision of adequate resources to conduct the research and so on. Such codes of practice are often a response to external concerns about accountability, efficiency and effectiveness in doctoral education. Typically these concerns reflect a broader challenge to universities to engage in new ways with industry and commerce and to respond to new forms of knowledge production and dissemination in an increasingly technology-driven globalised economy.

In the above scenario then, how is it best to approach the practice of doctoral supervision? A good starting point is to understand the policy drivers and contemporary circumstances in which doctoral education is embedded. Second, it is useful to analyse the way in which these circumstances play out in various practices and understandings of the project of doctoral education – particularly the supervisory role. Finally, it is important to develop the 'craft skills' of supervision and an approach to managing the supervisor–student relationship. Each of these will be dealt with in more detail below.

The Changing Conditions of Doctoral Education

Doctoral education has been increasingly the object of public scrutiny and policy debate in countries around the world. Two key drivers of this are first, the need for doctorates to support national innovation and economic development, and second, the growth and increasing diversity of the student population.

Innovation and Economic Development

In the US, the Council of Graduate Schools' White Paper, *A renewed commitment to graduate education* (2005), places doctoral education squarely within the economic agenda:

> The work of graduate students contributes directly to sustained economic growth, prosperity and national security. Graduate stu-

dents have gone on to conduct ground-breaking research in universities, national laboratories, and private industry. Many international students have remained in the U.S. and contributed to our scientific and technological accomplishments, while others have returned home to become national leaders and ambassadors for America . . . The United States is no longer attracting a sufficient number of highly qualified students into key research fields to develop the next generation of innovators and discoverers needed to sustain our economic leadership and national security into the 21st century. One key reason that this situation has emerged is that as a nation we are under-investing in research and human capital development. (p. 4)

The authors are particularly concerned with the competitive position of the US, remarking that 'Europe has now surpassed the U.S. in Science and Engineering Ph.D. production, and China is poised to do so within the next few years' (p. 4). To a large extent the growth in international students has offset the decline in domestic enrolments in the key areas of science, engineering and technology but now the capacity to attract international students is being threatened by 'changing visa requirements and negative perceptions of the US abroad' (p. 7). The report suggests a range of initiatives to address these problems such as:

- Improving participation and success, particularly among under-represented groups
- Stronger links between graduate schools and employers
- Promoting the development of flexible skills and the capacity to operate in interdisciplinary teams
- Funding to support more students in the key areas of science, technology, engineering and mathematics but including areas that promote global understanding of languages and culture
- Directing attention to programme quality.

In Europe the concerns are similar – the European Universities Association (EUA) has recently established the Council for Doctoral Education (CDE) which aims to improve Europe's research capacity and international competitiveness through providing a more structured approach to doctoral education: one which will allow more cooperation and the exchange of good practice.

The concern with employment, interdisciplinarity, flexible skills and innovation is arguably a response to the changing place of knowledge in contemporary society as depicted in the notion of the 'knowledge economy' (McWilliam & James, 2002). Harman (2002) argues that at the core of the knowledge economy are 'the ideas that future economic performance will be closely based on the skill and innovation level of the labour force, underpinned by effective research and R&D capacity' (p. 179). But the challenge for doctoral education is not simply to have more research students, more students engaged in the workplace and more industry-based research links (see Harman, 2002; Evans, 2002); rather, the challenge is located in the way in which the knowledge economy reconfigures both 'knowledge' and 'knowledge-workers'. The way in which it does so fundamentally challenges the idea of a university as a community of scholars working autonomously and adding to the stock of 'disciplinary' knowledge.

What then are some of the central features or claims made about the new 'knowledge-based' economy? The following list is one 'take' on these features:

1. Knowledge processes and products are central to success in the competitive environment of the new economy (Johnston, 2000; OECD, 2000; Allen Group, 2000).
2. Flexible and information-based technologies play a key role in generating and managing knowledge and in the emergence of knowledge based industries (Carnevale, 1991).
3. Knowledge, skill, creativity and enterprise are the key assets of the knowledge driven economy (Secretary of State for Trade and Industry, 1998; DISR, 2000; Kearns, 2001).
4. Knowledge workers, in addition to being innovative and enterprising, need to be able to locate performance within an understanding of organisational products and processes (Davenport & Prusack, 1998; McIntyre & Solomon, 2000).
5. The management of knowledge and knowledge workers is a new activity – it depends on linking people together, with continual learning and the renewal of ideas in flat and decentralised organisational structures (as Jack Welch, the former Chairman of GE notes 'Taking everyone's best ideas and transferring them to others is the secret. There is nothing more important ... and later ... Hierarchy is dead. The organisation of the future will be virtually layerless and increasingly boundaryless ...' Welch, 2001, p. 1).
6. Knowledge in the new economy is performance related and 'situated' in a particular context – thus it is not constrained within disciplinary boundaries.

Usher (2002) elaborates on the significance of the knowledge economy for doctoral education and universities more generally:

The first thing that can be said about this is that it replaces an epistemological with an economic definition of knowledge. Knowledge becomes a factor of production, more critical in the production process as economic performance comes to rely more and more heavily on knowledge inputs.

At the same time, the knowledge economy is one where knowledge is not only a key input but also an increasingly significant output that can be grown in an unlimited way . . . Economic growth is now seen to be vitally dependent on the development of an infrastructure that facilitates and enables sustainable knowledge development. (p. 144)

To this can be added a cluster of attributes said to characterise the new knowledge worker: innovative, flexible, multi-skilled, having a capacity to adapt to change, creative, entrepreneurial, collaborative, reflexive, having the ability to identify and solve problems, and the comportment of a lifelong learner (Edwards, Ranson & Strain, 2002). In the new knowledge economy, doctoral education becomes a site of tension on what constitutes legitimate knowledge, and on how the skills and attributes of the new knowledge worker are produced.

Growth and Diversity

In recent years much has been written about the increasing diversity of doctoral education (Pearson, 1999; Winter et al., 2000; Bourner et al., 2001; Usher, 2002; Tennant, 2004). There is diversity in the form of provision (such as the traditional PhD by thesis, professional doctorates and generic work-based doctorates), diversity within forms of provision (e.g. practice-based PhDs, PhDs by project, 'new route' PhDs, different mixes of course-work, artefact and thesis in professional doctorates) and diversity in the student population (increasing participation of women, more part-time students, greater age mix). In the US in 2008, the annual survey of graduate enrolment conducted by the Council of Graduate Schools in conjunction with the Graduate Record Examinations Board summarises the trend towards 'non-traditional' domestic graduate students since 1986: notably a growth in minority students at an average annual rate of 4–6% (African American, American Indian, Asian and Hispanic/Latino) with women accounting for the majority of growth. At the same time, white enrolment was unchanged (see Brown, 2006, p. 31).

In addition, overseas students make up 16% of the total graduate enrolment and 26% of graduate enrolment in designated research univer-sities. Nerad (2006) points to the increase in PhD production world-wide and to the growth in international students undertaking doctoral education. She reports the following percentages of earned doctoral degrees completed by international students in 2003: Germany 13%, Japan 13%, UK 39%, US 30%.

As McWilliam, Singh and Taylor (2002) comment, diversity is welcomed for both economic and social reasons, but it always brings with it fears and risks, especially relating to standards and quality:

> The aim is not to 'overcome' the diversity that is increasingly a feature of university student populations . . . the potential threat for universities as organizations lies not in diversity of student or staff populations but in systemic arbitrariness – in (inappropriate) organizational imprecision in the context of (appropriate) social imprecision. Put simply, the logic is that systems of management need to be uniform because individuals are not, nor are likely to be. (p. 123)

And so a uniformity of processes, procedures, standards and general outcomes will permit diversity in doctoral provision and in the population of doctoral candidates, while at the same time provide assurance about the nature and worthiness of a doctoral qualification.

In response to the economic imperative, the growth of enrolments and the need for diversity, there has been a more concerted effort by governments, accreditation agencies and peak bodies to regulate, control and/ or provide policy guidelines to universities, largely through more rigorous accreditation provisions, audit mechanisms, public reports and requirements relating to standards and quality assurance processes.

Contributing to a major UNESCO comparative study of doctoral education in Europe and the US, Kehm (2004) summarises what she sees as the trend in the 13 countries represented in a major UNESCO study of doctoral education:

> The trend . . . is to establish a relatively formal structure for Doctoral education, ie abolishing the traditional 'apprenticeship model', consisting of a professorial supervisor and independent research, in favour of more structured research education and training within disciplinary or interdisciplinary programmes or graduate schools. (p. 283)

Taken together, the 'economic' and 'growth and diversity' drivers have fostered a general concern with employment outcomes, global competitiveness, economic success, the need to prepare doctoral graduates for participation in a global knowledge-based society, the need for interdisciplinary research, increased participation, encouraging and responding to diverse and growing student populations, ensuring quality processes and outcomes and improved efficiency and effectiveness including improved retention rates and a reduction in the time it takes to complete a PhD.

In various ways all these concerns exert their influence on the project of doctoral education and the roles and practices of doctoral supervision.

The Project of Doctoral Education and the Supervisory Role

Yeatman (1995) argues that the traditional model for the doctoral student supervision relationship has been the master–apprentice model whereby the mysteries of the craft are revealed to the apprentice who is inducted into an academic scholarly and research culture. She is critical of this traditional relationship as being governed by a narrative of scholarly genius where the apprentice (or perhaps more accurately the 'disciple') demonstrates his or her worth: 'The heroic quality of the supervisor is echoed in and attested to by the heroic quality of the supervisee, especially once the latter has passed the final test, the submission' (p. 9). Such a relationship, she argues, is highly privatised, paternalistic and governed by implicit norms that are not open to public scrutiny and accountability. She calls for this traditional relationship to be abandoned, and for the establishment of a more systematic and managed approach to graduate supervision pedagogy. She does so on the basis of government concerns for efficiency and effectiveness, and the growth and diversity of the student population. As she remarks, the traditional model is 'inadequate to the needs of many new PhD aspirants who, by historical-cultural positioning, have not been invited to imagine themselves as subjects of genius' (p. 9).

But there are other compelling reasons to abandon the traditional model. Johnson, Lee and Green (2000), for example, problematise a core idea embedded in the traditional model: the notion of the 'independent, autonomous scholar' as the exemplary outcome of the doctoral education process. They point to an alternative image of the scholar based on new modes of knowledge production (see Gibbons et al., 1994) appropriate to the new knowledge economy:

> a new figure of the scholar would appear to be more appropriate to forms of research training associated with new modes of knowledge production ... researchers who are skilled in collaboration, in the recognition of the interdependence of human relations, and in the appreciation of the concrete skills and specific capacities of others ... Research training to provide scholars able to work in these new ways will require students to develop sensitivities to the concerns of others, a willingness to work with others, and a capacity to reason or make judgements on the basis of contextual information rather than relying purely on abstract, universalising principles. (p. 146)

In this scenario the supervisor is not a 'master' but a teacher of certain skills, capacities and ways of conducting oneself in a scholarly research environment. In this way the 'curriculum' of doctoral study goes beyond the production of a dissertation and indeed beyond the supervisory relationship. Most universities provide additional supports for doctoral students: seminars, workshops developing broader research and scholarly skills, access to online resources and so on; but these have primarily been seen as additional or complementary to the main task of the doctoral student: to produce a dissertation. Nowadays, however, the development of broadbased skills has become more central and formalised, being expressed variously as 'attributes', 'competencies' or 'skills'.

A good example of this can be found in the UK 'Joint Statement by Research Councils/Arts and Humanities Research Board (AHRB)'. This document specifies the skills that doctoral research students would be expected to develop during their research training – what are often referred to as 'generic skills'. These comprise 35 separately listed skills, styled 'to be able to . . .', and categorised under the following headings:

1. Research skills and techniques e.g. to be able to demonstrate original, independent and critical thinking.
2. Research environment e.g. to be able to understand the processes for funding and evaluation of research.
3. Research management e.g. to be able to apply effective project management through the setting of research goals, intermediate milestones and prioritisation of activities.
4. Personal effectiveness e.g. to be able to demonstrate flexibility and open-mindedness.
5. Communication skills e.g. to be able to write clearly and in a style appropriate to purpose.
6. Networking and teamworking e.g. to be able to develop and maintain cooperative networks, working relationships with supervisors, colleagues and peers, within the institution and wider research community.
7. Career management e.g. to be able to appreciate the need and show commitment to continued professional development.

(QAAHE, 2004, pp. 34–35)

Clearly many of these skills can be developed and/or demonstrated outside the supervisory relationship and through practices other than completing a dissertation. In a study of the experiences of doctoral students, Cumming (2008) identifies the constellation of individuals, other than candidates and supervisors, who are potentially engaged in the activities of a doctoral candidate. These include a range of academics within and outside the department and university, professionals, business and industry contacts, community members, online contacts, peers, technicians, librarians, industry researchers, other candidates and postdoctoral researchers; in addition to the network of associates, friends, partners and family. To this range of participants in the doctoral enterprise should be added the various community agencies, institutions, organisations, networks and resources that may come into play; and finally, there are the structures, regulations, cultures and infrastructure of the academy.

> Rather than situate the candidate and/or supervisor at the centre of a constellation of others – in the sense of occupying a predetermined or fixed position – it is proposed that individuals engaged in doctoral activity be considered as part of an open and flexible system. Conceptualised in this way, individuals can be seen as in a constant state of flux, moving and establishing a multitude of links over time. (p. 91)

Cumming makes the point that we need to understand how our doctoral practices sit inside a host of links with other participants, the academy and the community. He categorises doctoral practices into curriculum, pedagogy, research and work. Curricular practices have to do with negotiating the topic and field of study, the problems that need investigating, the framing of a problem to be investigated and the design of a study. They include intellectual engagement with academic, professional and industry or community perspectives on the problem; the kinds of skills and attributes being developed over the candidature; the use of the results for commercial or other purposes; and career possibilities upon completion. Pedagogical practices have to do with the processes and activities the candidate engages in to advance their work. These include meetings with supervisors and other advisers, how they interact with 'stakeholders' in the doctoral candidature, networking activities, presenting conference papers, seminar attendance and presentations, attending workshops and training sessions, engagement in online discussions, etc. Research practices include reviewing the literature, research design, generating data, analysing data, writing, theorising and complying with institutional requirements such as intellectual property, safety and ethics. Work practices include teaching, publishing, preparing grant applications, negotiating patents, balancing the needs and expectations of industry and academic partners, delivering talks to community groups and participating in academic governance. Cumming's model of the doctoral enterprise is depicted in Figure 10.1.

In this model, supervisors, like candidates, are no longer centre stage. Instead they need to understand themselves in relation to a complex and shifting set of doctoral arrangements and practices. This immediately raises questions about the role of the supervisor and the skills needed to undertake this role. Clearly supervisors represent the academy and its culture, regulations and structures. They are also engaged in discussion with industry partners and outside organisations and agencies that have

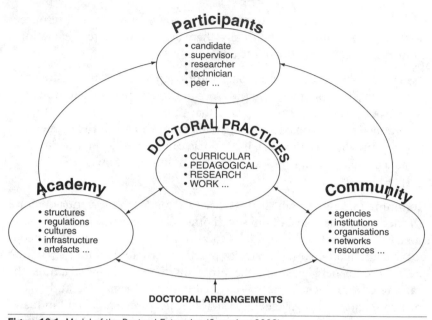

Figure 10.1 Model of the Doctoral Enterprise (Cumming, 2008)
Reproduced with permission from Jim Cumming

an interest in the study. So, too, are they involved in negotiations and discussions with a range of individuals who have some stake in the research, such as technicians and other academics. Supervisors may also take on responsibility for developing the broader employment-related skills of candidates and be mindful of their role in addressing the range of contemporary concerns about doctoral education.

As such supervisors can be seen as managers of a very complex and ambiguous enterprise. This is the approach adopted by Vilkinas (1998), who uses the literature in leadership and management to understand the complexity of the supervisory role. She identifies nine management roles that supervisors need to develop and adopt as the circumstances warrant. Table 10.1 outlines these roles with some comments linking them to Cumming's model of the doctoral enterprise.

The model of Cumming and the supervisory roles of Vilkinas provides a good map of the kinds of arrangements, practices and interventions in which supervisors engage. Categorising the roles in this way is really a heuristic device which brings out the complexity and diversity of the doctoral enterprise and hopefully assists supervisors to better understand the scope and nature of the supervisory relationship and the skills they need for effective intervention.

Table 10.1 Supervisory Roles

Supervisory roles	Characteristics	Comment
Innovator	Flexible and creative. Looks for new ways to do things. Takes a different angle on a problem. Willing to experiment.	This role fits in well with curricular doctoral practices. It is useful at the beginning of the candidature in setting up the problem being addressed. It may also be useful when the candidate becomes stuck on some obstacle.
Broker	Secures resources. Introduces students to networks. Influences industry and/or the department.	The supervisor engages here with other participants (e.g. other academics, technicians or department heads) and negotiates with industry or community partners.
Producer	Focuses on the product and the steps needed to complete the dissertation.	This is a doctoral practice very much focused on the research – its design, reporting and analysis. The focus is often on producing written material (e.g. a literature review, a methodology chapter or the work practice of producing a publication).
Director	Plans, prioritises and provides clarification and structure.	Here the supervisor takes on the role of project manager, refocusing the project and its core aims and what needs to be done. The emphasis is often on curricular and research practices.
Coordinator	Can anticipate and plan for workflow problems. Links the timing and importance of different activities.	The supervisor coordinates different elements of the research – planning ahead and managing risks. This requires an understanding of the needs and expectations of different parties to the study – the academy, the community and participants.
Monitor	Evaluates progress – holds regular reviews, etc.	This role relates to the structures, regulations and culture of the academy. The supervisor ensures that reports on progress are well maintained and that the research complies with relevant policies.
Facilitator	Helps students to develop the range of skills necessary to complete a dissertation. Provides encouragement and fosters teamwork.	The supervisor focuses on the pedagogical doctoral practices (e.g. regular meetings, seminars, writing groups, attendance at workshops, fosters engagement in teams, etc.).

(*Continued overleaf*)

Table 10.1 Continued

Supervisory roles	Characteristics	Comment
Mentor	Understands the needs of the students and provides pastoral care.	Ensures that students undertake work practices that are congruent with their career aspirations and that they have appropriate work skills.
Integrator	Looks broadly at the supervisory process and its strengths and weaknesses in relation to what is needed. Capacity to diagnose problems and move between roles when needed.	This is where the supervisor steps back and looks at all the doctoral practices and arrangements that are in play. This is done in the context of the wider agendas in doctoral education, evident in emerging policies, practices and scholarship.

Source: After Vilkinas, 1998

The Supervisory Relationship and Supervision Skills

Ironically, the broader conception of research education presented above, in which the supervisor is located within a web of other arrangements and practices, actually demands that supervisors expand their repertoire of skills. In addition to the normal scholarly and research skills, they may be called upon to provide advice on research commercialisation, intellectual property, risk management, ethics, safety, publishing, the development of employment-related skills, work-based or industry-linked research, inter-disciplinary research and professional and academic networking. They also need to be mindful of the broader policy and institutional issues and requirements, such as rules and regulations regarding admission, progress and examination, and the way in which issues such as quality assurance, diversity, the need for completions and research outcomes are played out at institutional level.

Rather than go through an exhaustive list of skills, the remainder of this chapter will outline some of the considerations that need to be addressed in the early stages of candidature. A report on doctoral education in a UK-based newspaper, the *Independent*, is a reminder of the importance of the early stages of candidature and the persistence of the centrality of the supervisor to student success.

Laura began a PhD in Chinese cultural studies in 2003, but within months realised that something was wrong. "After six months, I became worried. I had only met my supervisor once, and I seemed to have no plan or sense of direction," she says. "Although my department had seemed delighted to accept me as a PhD student – even awarding me a studentship – it soon became clear that my supervisors knew nothing about my subject. I began to realise that the only reason my department had taken me on was to broaden their research profile."

Things deteriorated rapidly. Her supervisor showed no interest in her work, and communication broke down completely. Despite repeated complaints to her department, nothing was done to resolve the situation.

(Lynch, 2008)

What then makes for a successful candidature, and what can the supervisor do early in the candidature to increase the likelihood of success?

In a wide-ranging review of the literature Latona and Browne (2001) identified factors that had an impact on the likelihood of successful completion of a research degree. They grouped these factors into three broad categories: institutional and environmental factors, individual supervisory arrangements and student cohorts and characteristics. The institutional and environmental factors include disciplinary differences (e.g. that science students typically work within a tightly knit group of researchers while humanities students tend to work solely with their supervisor), the establishment of structured milestones throughout candidature and the critical importance of the sense of belonging to a group or a research culture. Individual supervisory arrangements include the timeliness and fit for purpose feedback from supervisors, the frequency of meetings and structure of activities between meetings, the existence of negotiated supervision protocols that address expectations and needs, the quality of the relationship with the supervisor, continuity in topic and supervisor and getting started and committing early to a project. And finally student cohorts and characteristics include entry qualifications (first class honours is important for science students but does not predict success for arts and humanities students), part- or full-time study, financial security and psychological factors such as a tendency to procrastination.

Ives and Rowley (2005) comment on the importance of matching students and supervisors. The three most important factors in a successful match being academic area (i.e. supervisor's expertise aligns with student's topic), the matching of interpersonal working patterns and a match in research methodology.

Some supervisors and students were willing to accept a high match in two areas and sacrifice the third. The area that most supervisors were willing to sacrifice was the match in methodology, whereas students were more willing to sacrifice the topic. Arguments for sacrificing the match regarding topic were that you need some

> knowledge, but do not need to be an expert. Arguments for sacrificing the methodology match were that you can involve someone else in this part of the supervision if needed. Both groups thought the match in interpersonal working patterns was critical. (p. 541)

This view of the centrality of a good interpersonal working relationship is compatible with the findings of others and with the testimonies of experienced supervisors (see Fraser & Mathews, 1999).

Although the above observations are not exhaustive, they provide a good general starting point for establishing an effective supervisory relationship. Such a relationship needs to take into account factors relating variously to the student, the supervisor and the organisational climate.

Factors Related to Students

Academic Capacity

It is important to understand as much of the background of the student in the early stage of candidature. The most obvious factor is the student's prior qualifications and experience that equips them for research. It is not always possible to ascertain this from the submitted paperwork, especially when making a judgement about academic equivalences from degrees earned overseas or even degrees earned at other domestic universities. Universities source their research students from at least three areas: their own undergraduate and masters students, graduates of other domestic universities and graduates from overseas universities. In all cases it is imperative that you sight some work of the candidate – whether this is their honours thesis, a research report or an extended proposal for research. A particularly sensitive case arises when a student is taken on after a period of supervision with another supervisor. The difficulty here is to make an assessment of the student's progress and potential to complete without compromising academic colleagues who may have had previous involvement in the project. This is generally not an issue in the US, whereby universities typically admit candidates to the dissertation phase after the completion of coursework and a general examination.

Research Topic

The research topic needs to be sufficiently thought through to provide the teacher with a basis for making a decision to be part of the project. Irrespective of whether there is a formal institutional requirement to submit a proposal with an application it is a good idea to insist on this prior to taking on a student – this can be done in the stage leading up to the student making an application. Analysing a proposal provides a great deal of information about the student's theoretical and methodological perspective, writing style, general approach to research and, even, motive for undertaking the research. It also provides information about the resources that will be needed to sustain and support the research.

Students' Needs, Motives and Expectations

Students' needs, motives and expectations can really only be explored through face-to-face or telephone contact. This discussion should include an assessment of what you can offer as a supervisor and what the institution can offer to support the project. It is always useful to ask questions about both short-term motives for undertaking the proposed research and longer-term career motives for enrolling in a research degree. For example, the research itself may be motivated by a personal or professional concern, by a gap in the literature or simply by intellectual curiosity. This may or may not make a difference to how you supervise, depending on your approach to research and what constitutes a 'legitimate' problem for investigation. For example, if the topic is motivated by a professional concern then it is more than likely to be a multidisciplinary study, but not all supervisors are comfortable supervising such projects. As far as longer-term career aspirations are concerned, students invariably see supervisors as mentors in a broader sense and they look to them for guidance on the strategies and skills needed to pursue a research career either inside or outside the academy – they may be interested in developing skills such as writing articles for publication, delivering conference papers, understanding the research commercialisation process and so on.

Preferred Working Style

As mentioned above, matching interpersonal working styles is quite crucial for successful candidature. The best way to diagnose the preference of the student is to talk with them about how they worked with a previous supervisor, say the supervisor of their honours thesis if applicable. It may also be worth going systematically through an instrument such as Gurr's (2001) Student–Supervisor Alignment Tool Kit. In the Ives and Rowley (2005) study those students who were initially satisfied but became dissatisfied later in their candidature reported that the reason for their dissatisfaction was insufficient guidance, feedback and structure from their supervisors. This is an ironic finding since the need for guidance, feedback and structure should ideally diminish over the candidature. It is important, therefore, to accurately describe and discuss your actual supervision practices rather than your 'preferred' practices, and any anticipated change in those practices over the span of the project. A good question to pose is to consider who is the project director. Is the supervisor the director or the student? If the student, then is the supervisor equivalent to a chair of an advisory committee? Discussions such as these typically draw out perspectives and views that would remain unanalysed until such time as they caused tension in the student–supervisor relationship.

Factors Related to the Supervisor

Motives, Demands, Expectations

In engaging with a potential student it is important to acknowledge your own motives. Why have you taken on the role of research student supervisor? Is it simply a professional obligation? Are you motivated by the topic being proposed? Is the student work part of a research project or overall research plan that you are pursuing in the academic unit? Are research student completions necessary for your research profile and perhaps promotion or subsequent appointment? Are you interested in the process of research supervision and research training and its role in building a research culture? Are you interested in the overall skills development of your student or is your sole focus the production of a thesis? Do you simply enjoy one-to-one supervision sessions as a form of teaching? No doubt many academics will identify with more than one of the above and indeed the predominant motive may differ between students. Differing motives lead to subtly different expectations of students. For example, if the student is on a scholarship that has been provided by a grant that you have received from an industry source you will need to balance the demands placed on the student with the demands placed on you from the project steering committee. If the project has commercial potential you will need to address the implications with the student prior to agreeing to supervise.

Conception of Research and Model of Supervision

It is important to analyse and articulate the conception of research that you hold and the model of supervision that drives your demands and expectations of the student. Earlier in this chapter, we explored articles on research supervision that advanced supervisor–student relationships other than the historically dominant master–apprentice model. To expand on this, Johnson et al. (2000) quote from one of their interviewees in their study – a person who had been supervised at Oxford University and was modelling her supervisory practices on her experiences at Oxford:

'There was no student whose thesis I read in full. And I told them at the beginning. And I said I'm not going to be reading more than half of this and if you are uneasy about that, I won't supervise you. I will recommend someone else. Because it is more than about . . . it is more than just writing a thesis. It's about learning to be independent. And I think that's one of the great things in scholarship, learning . . . but it's tough, you've got to learn to rely on your own judgement and not to run to the supervisor for every problem that you have. And that's the test in the end. And you can fail it.' (p. 137)

They report her as indicating that it was an Oxford rule that no supervisor was to read more than half the thesis. Her own supervisor explained the rule as: 'the reason is that we want to be quite clear in our own minds and we want the student to be quite clear that it is their work' (p. 137).

This is at the other end of the spectrum to the model being advocated by the contemporary concern for outputs, with a corresponding emphasis on 'time to complete', 'retention to completion' and indicators of quality supervision. McCormack (2004) observes that such concerns lead to a linear model of supervision as structured and progressing in a step-like manner – a kind of project management approach to supervision. The point she makes is that whatever your model of supervision, addressing any discrepancies with students is important at the beginning of candidature – preferably as part of the process of agreeing to supervise.

Strengths and Weaknesses

An honest appraisal of your own strengths and weaknesses, mapped against the needs of the potential student and the skills of any co-supervisor or supervisory panel, will greatly assist the process of establishing a good supervisory relationship. The strengths and weaknesses may relate to academic matters such as theoretical knowledge of the area, practical knowledge of research techniques and methodologies, a knowledge of the relevant literature, the ability to supervise across disciplinary areas; or to non-academic matters such as taking the initiative in making appointments with students, providing written feedback on all submitted work, arranging for students to give conference or seminar papers or arranging the purchase of necessary equipment and so on. The question really is 'How can I help this student as a supervisor with the knowledge, skills and predispositions that I know I have?' This, of course, needs to be asked in the context of co-supervisors and any willingness you may have to develop new skills and dispositions as a matter for your own professional development.

An important area to consider is your capacity to work with others in the supervision of a particular student. Where the co-supervisor has already been appointed or supervisory panel has already been formed then an assessment of your capacity to collaborate with the team is crucial.

Organisational Factors

As argued above the contemporary circumstances of higher education have led to policy shifts in research and research training that have found their way into university policies and procedures. There is a concern with timely completions and the reduction of waste in the system (see, for example, the PhD Completion Project (2008) being conducted by the Council of Graduate Schools in the US, which show seven-year completion rates of only 45–47% for local students). One common institutional response has been a renewed emphasis on improving the quality of the research student experience. Three particular aspects of quality are the monitoring of supervisor performance, the provision of opportunities for students to develop broad based skills that will stand them in good stead in seeking employment and the provision of sufficient resources and support for students so they are retained and complete on time. All these aspects have implications for the decision to supervise particular students. For example, if supervisor performance is measured by the number of on-time completions then this would drive supervisors to only take on the very best students. On the other hand, if supervisor performance were measured by student satisfaction or by some measure of 'value add' then supervisors would be motivated to take on more 'non-traditional' students. This is not to deny the social justice motives of supervisors, only to point out the consequences of misplaced policies. On the issue of developing broad based skills – if the student is seeking this then you should be mindful of the university provision for this. If there is little institutional provision then the burden of provision will fall on your shoulders, so an assessment of this is important. Finally, with respect to general support you should be aware that across the sector this has been an area of student dissatisfaction, a dissatisfaction that will have an impact on your supervisory relationship. Apart from financial and physical resources a valuable resource is the research climate in the academic unit. This is a great source of potential support for you as a supervisor. Prior to taking on a supervisory role you should be satisfied that the support students expect and/or require is available. If not then you will need to address their unrealistic expectations or decline to supervise.

In summary, supervision means taking on a research project and an intense teaching responsibility that may extend for four or more years. It is certainly worth exploring, then, the precursors to agreeing to supervise. This chapter analyses some of the factors to consider when deciding whether to supervise a particular student. The factors relating to students include their background, their motives for undertaking a doctorate, their capabilities, needs, expectations, resources and personal styles. Supervisors, for their part, need to be mindful of their motives, demands, expectations and strengths and weaknesses in relation to particular students being considered for supervision. Supervision, of course, does not exist in a vacuum and so contextual factors also play a part, such as the way in which performance as a supervisor is measured in the department, the need to work with co-supervisors or supervisory panels and the broader policy framework within which supervision occurs.

Enhancing Professional Practice

Exercise 1 – Understanding Your Strengths, Weaknesses and Values in the Supervision Process

For each of the items below please rate:

- your skills and knowledge
- the importance of each item to you.

Please note that the focus of the items is on the process of supervision rather than on your research and scholarly expertise. Once you have completed the rating please compare your 'importance' results with colleagues and identify and discuss any discrepancies. The purpose of the exercise is to clarify your conception of your role and to identify your strengths and weaknesses.

Table 10.2 Diagnosing Strengths, Weaknesses and Values as a Supervisor

Item	Rating	Importance
	Low 1 2 3 4 5 High	Low 1 2 3 4 5 High
A familiarity with published work on the process of research supervision		
An understanding of the external policy environment in research education		
Well networked in a global academic community		
An understanding of university regulations, requirements and processes in relation to doctoral candidature		
Knowledge of the support available for the project within the university		
Knowledge of the broader university support available for the candidate (e.g. seminars, peer support, writing workshops)		

(Continued overleaf)

Table 10.2 Continued

Item	Rating	Importance
	Low 1 2 3 4 5 High	Low 1 2 3 4 5 High
Supervising across a broad range of topics		
Supervising interdisciplinary dissertations		
Supervising industry and/or work-based research		
Keeping records of meetings and actions taken		
An understanding of the commercialistion process		
Knowledge of the career pathways available to students		
Introducing students to academic networks within and beyond the university		
Integrating students into the intellectual life of the university		
Balancing encouragement and support with honest feedback on work		
Assisting students with their writing skills		
Working with students from diverse backgrounds		
Advising on the literature review		
Generating creative original ideas relating to the problem or methodology		
Discussing the issues and concerns of the student that affect their progress		
Monitoring progress		
Integrating students into research teams		
Project management skills		
Gauging the needs and motives of students		
Assisting candidates with seminar and conference presentations		

Exercise 2 – Communicating Your Approach to Supervision

Prepare a short description of your approach to supervision and research. Write it as though it were part of a website that prospective students could access. You might like to mention the qualities you look for in students, what you expect of them, what they can expect from you, how you like to run meetings and the activities and outcomes you hope to achieve with the students.

Swap descriptions with one or more colleagues and discuss differences and commonalities. Revise you description following your discussion with colleagues.

CHAPTER 11

Teaching and Research

Introduction

Ronald Barnett (2005) opens his book titled *Reshaping the university: New relationships between research, scholarship and teaching* with the lament:

> The debate as to the relationship between teaching and research is surely already becoming tired, if not tiresome. Opponents barely confront each other's arguments, tending rather to speak past each other. (p. 1)

Keeping Barnett's words in mind, this chapter is not so much directed at entering into this debate with a view to offering some kind of resolution, but to understanding the debate and its impact on the professional identities of academics.

It only takes a short time in academic life to witness the contestation between teaching and research. The contestation is apparent in academic meetings of various kinds and is often sparked by the disquiet some academics feel about additional resources being targeted towards research at the 'expense' of teaching. They typically make the observation that teaching is the core function of the university and its principal source of revenue, and during periods of financial constraint they ask 'Can we afford to invest precious dollars in research when student–staff ratios are so high, when teaching infrastructure needs upgrading and when new courses need to be mounted?' To which the predictable reply comes 'The question is not whether we can afford to invest in research, the question is whether we can afford not to do so', accompanied by an appeal to the reputational value of research and the necessity of having research active staff in teaching positions to ensure quality and standards. Another site where contestation is apparent is in annual promotional or tenure rounds. At such times the common belief expressed is that research has higher status as an indicator of academic excellence and is therefore more likely to be rewarded than a lifetime of dedicated teaching, course development and course administration. This view seems to be impervious to the attempts by academic managers to assure staff that all aspects of academic life are taken into account by promotion and tenure committees – that is, research and scholarship, teaching and service to the university and the community. At its worst the contestation becomes personal, with those who feel disenfranchised by their commitment to teaching remarking on the well-resourced and privileged life that 'researchers' lead, and researchers, for their part, remarking on the failure of 'teachers' to contribute to the research effort of the academic unit. This, of course, is in the context where all staff are expected to undertake both teaching and research.

The way language is used in this debate is also instructive. For example, we speak of academics who are 'research active', with the primary measure of activity being quantitative: how many research grants? For how much money? How many books and articles published? How many doctoral students supervised to completion? But it makes no sense to talk of someone as 'teaching active' in the same way. This is because we want to know how well the person teaches – knowing the number of classes and class sizes is not sufficient for us to make a judgement about the quality of teaching. Of course we are also interested in the quality of research, but this is built into standard, globally recognised indicators of research: the ability to win research grants, to publish books with recognised publishers and articles in refereed journals and to supervise doctoral students to completion. Then there is the widespread practice of 'buying out' of teaching or having teaching loads reduced under various circumstances such as when a research grant is awarded, when a contract is won for a non-research purpose or when an academic takes on an academic management role. Once again there is no equivalent expression for research: the idea of 'buying out' of research is not entertained. Teaching is thus the default activity of academics – when they are not undertaking funded research or other approved activities then they must do a full teaching load. An extension of this is the view, often held among academic managers, that those staff who are not research active should undertake increased teaching loads. Thus teaching is positioned as a punishment.

I make these introductory comments to illustrate that any enquiry into the relationship between teaching and research can hardly be said to be neutral and disinterested – it is an emotionally laden, highly contested and sometimes very personalised terrain. This may go some way to explaining Barnett's observation of the seemingly intractable positions held by those with opposing views on the relationship. Having said this, we now turn to the way in which the relationship has been depicted in the scholarly literature.

Empirical Studies, Models and Myths

Is there evidence that teaching and research are linked, and, if so, in what way are they linked? We draw here on two meta-analyses of the literature: that of Hattie and Marsh (1996) which reviewed 58 studies, and that of Hughes (2005) who reviewed articles published in four leading refereed journals in the period 1990–2002 (*Higher Education, Higher Education Quarterly, Higher Education Review* and *Studies in Higher Education*).

Hattie and Marsh (1996) grouped these models into three broad arguments: those that postulate a negative relationship, a positive relationship or a zero relationship between teaching and research, as shown in Table 11.1.

Table 11.1 Models of the Relationship between Teaching and Research

Relationship	Model
Negative	**Scarcity model** – where an academic's limited resources of time, energy and commitment are insufficient to be productive in both teaching and research. In an early study Ramsden and Moses (1992) found that teaching and research were not mutually beneficial. Rather than being complementary they were likely to be in conflict with each other. Indeed the separation of teaching and research may improve the quality of teaching as, 'The weak researchers would be freed from the distractions of attempting to do something they were inexpert at doing' (p. 294).
	Differential personality model – which proposes that the two activities require different personal dispositions, for example, that the personal disposition of researchers is to work alone and to be comfortable working with ideas and facts within a disciplinary field whereas teachers are more gregarious and like interacting with students to explore ideas.
	Divergent reward system model – where the two activities constitute different roles that are rewarded differently and therefore in a constant state of tension. There is very little empirical research relating to this, but what there is allows Hattie and Marsh to observe that teaching is less likely to contribute to overall salary than research.

(Continued overleaf)

Table 11.1 Continued

Relationship	Model
Positive	**Conventional wisdom model** – this refers to the common belief among academics that teaching and research are positively related. This commonsense belief is founded on the idea that research is good for teaching – it is important for disseminating advanced knowledge, for keeping academics rejuvenated and contemporary, and for maintaining the reputation of the academic unit. But the positive influence is mainly considered to be a one-way affair, with research activity improving teaching and not the other way around.
	The generic underlying ability model – this model posits that there is a common set of abilities underlying teaching and research, such as commitment, creativity, an investigative spirit and a capacity for critical analysis.
Zero	**The different enterprises model** – this model contends that research is knowledge in the context of discovery while teaching is knowledge in the context of transmission. In addition, research exists in the public domain while teaching is largely private and its impact is judged differently.
	The unrelated personality model – this is the opposite of the 'differential personality' model, claiming instead that researchers and teachers have very few personal attributes in common. Hattie and Marsh (1996) precis the early work of Rushton, Murray and Paunonen (1983): 'Researchers are more likely to be ambitious, enduring, seeking definiteness, dominant, showing leadership, aggressive, independent, not meek, and nonsupportive. Teachers are liberal, sociable, showing leadership, extroverted, low in anxiety, objective, supportive, nonauthoritarian, not defensive' (p. 514).
	The bureaucratic funding model – this model sees the very different funding arrangements for teaching and research at the systemic and individual university level as evidence of the bureaucratic view that research and teaching are not related

Source: After Hattie and Marsh, 1996

On the basis of empirical evidence or the lack thereof, Hattie and Marsh conclude that the relationship between teaching and research is zero. Following his review of key journals, Hughes (2005) agrees, concluding that there is no empirical evidence to support the existence of a relationship between teaching and learning: 'What emerges from this literature is a sense that the anticipated empirical evidence to support the existence of teaching and research relationships does not exist' (p. 15). But what they both found is that the models and myths put forward about the relationship are well entrenched. Hughes then goes on to treat the various myths in circulation about this relationship saying, 'The mythology may be

Table 11.2 The Mythology of Research and Teaching Relationships in Universities

Myths	Hughes' comments
That there is a mutually beneficial relationship	'The essence of this myth is that there is an empirically proven, mutually beneficial relationship between research and teaching' (Hughes, 2005, p. 24). Despite the lack of empirical evidence, there is an enduring belief that teaching and research are mutually beneficial.
That there is a generalisable and static relationship	But research and teaching are dynamic and evolving and highly context dependent.
That scholarship is separate from research and teaching	Scholarship can be understood as 'new and critical interpretations of what is already known' (Elton, 1992, quoted in Hughes, 2005, p. 20) and it is arguably central to both teaching and research. But scholarship rarely appears as central to the mission statements of universities, which mainly focus on teaching and research.
That lectures who are researchers are superior teachers	The argument is that there is evidence that lecturers who are researchers are better than those who are not researchers.
That research into the relationship between research and teaching is disinterested	Hughes points out that this is highly unlikely since there is so much vested interest among those who carry out research into the teaching and research relationship.

Source: After Hughes, 2005

explained in terms of the misinterpretation of the available evidence, mystification of the debate and mischief of the protagonists' (p. 16). The myths he identifies are summarised in Table 11.2 above.

But why do the myths persist? Perhaps because the real nature of the relationship is unknowable in any global sense and because there are competing vested interests at the systemic, institutional and individual levels.

The Dual Economy of Research and Teaching

Scott (2005) refers to the dual economy in higher education: one for teaching and one for research. The split between teaching and research is enshrined at the highest level of government where ministerial portfolios for education are typically separated from those relating to research. For example, in Australia there is a Minister for Education and a Minister for Innovation, Industry, Science and Research. These ministries have separate bureaucracies that fund, monitor and report on education and research respectively. Respectively, it is the Department of Education, Employment and Workplace Relations (DEEWR) for education and the Australian Research Council (ARC) and National Health and Medical Research Council (NH&MRC) for research. Not surprisingly this separation is imitated in university portfolios and structures throughout Australia – typically there is a deputy vice-chancellor for research and a separate deputy vice-chancellor for education or 'teaching and learning' with separate budgets and separate key performance indicators. In turn, university level structures are typically mirrored in the structure of faculties of schools – with academic managers occupying the different portfolios of research and teaching (e.g. associate deans – research or teaching). Promotion criteria also separate these two fundamental aspects of university life and so individual CVs and performance plans do the same. This scenario is mirrored around the world.

It is interesting to note that teaching and research are also measured in very different ways: instruments designed to measure the quality of courses and teaching rarely mention research, and measures of research almost never refer to teaching quality. In addition the half-life of 'teaching performance' is much shorter than the half-life of research performance. A publication in a refereed journal maintains its currency in an individual academic's 'research record' but a favourable report on teaching is unlikely to carry currency after 20 years or so. At the institutional level too the various national and global league tables provide no measure of the relationship – research and teaching metrics are always separated. An obvious metric would be citations of articles in course materials to look at the impact of research on teaching programmes.

Notwithstanding all this institutional separation individual academics are then encouraged to 'integrate' their teaching and research so that they are complementary aspects of the same activity of being an academic! Most academics occupy this hybrid space, and struggle with it.

Convergent and Divergent Trends in the Teaching and Research Relationship

Hughes makes the point that each of the terms of the relationship 'teaching' and 'research' are not singular and static – instead they change over time and are highly context dependent. For example, research processes in the natural sciences are very different from those in the social sciences and humanities, and teaching varies greatly between discipline areas, level of study and mode of delivery. In addition teaching and research change over time. And yet the question about the relationship between research and teaching is always framed in a global way, as if research and teaching were distinct and known entities – but how we conceive of each is crucial to the debate, and how each is influenced by broader changes is relevant. For example, Naidoo (2005) makes the point that the incursion of market forces into higher education serves to commodify higher education which changes how we position teaching and research. As commodities they are conceived in terms of their exchange value in the marketplace. She goes on to argue that:

> the reshaping of research and teaching to fit the requirements of the market place are also likely to tear apart the two activities . . . the transition of research and teaching from 'a comfortable relationship' to one of 'mutual antagonism' (Barnett 2003, 157) may shift to a third phase where the necessity or even possibility of linking pedagogy and research simply withers away. (p. 30)

What counts as valuable research has been reconfigured to place greater emphasis on its commercial value and its impact on industry with attendant interests in patenting and 'commercial in confidence' transactions that take research out of the public realm and arguably compromises the critical independent stance of researchers so valued in former times.

As mentioned in Chapter 1, the commodification of teaching and learning leads to a conceptualisation of the relationship between academics and students as one of a service provider and consumer – and there have been various levers used to increase the 'student as consumer' ethic (student feedback, fees). Learning resources are increasingly being standardised.

> This can also represent and attempt to 'teacher proof' delivery, particularly if institutions are planning to use 'cheaper' staff . . . In this standardized model of teaching, activities through which teachers adjust the curriculum and pedagogy to the needs of individual students, as well as peer-group learning, tend to be overlooked. (Naidoo, 2005, p. 32)

A consumerist framework also entails more administration, marketing and monitoring so that the emphasis is on documenting, accounting and measuring rather than developing innovative high-quality academic programmes.

On this account it could be argued that teaching and research are coming together under the common umbrella of tradeable commodities in the global marketplace. In such a regime there is an emphasis on the dissemination of research and the need for an awareness of the impact of research. Teaching can form an alliance with research in this sense. There is also the growing need for graduates to have research skills as an important part of their employability. And it is certainly true that industry partners are completely indifferent to the teaching and research wars being raged in universities – their focus on outcomes allows them to see past all that. Against this trend Scott (2005) argues that:

> Individual careers – the idea of the teaching and research academic is being superseded by more focused professional identities – learning and teaching 'experts' and research only staff – there has been a separate development of both teaching and research as evident by the professionalisation of both functions plus the interpenetration of teaching and research in intellectual terms. (p. 53)

And so the general scenario he sees (admittedly too simplistically) is a separation of teaching and research in policy and political terms, and a convergence in intellectual terms. The convergence in intellectual terms can be seen in the notion of 'knowledge work' where the separate categories of research, teaching and learning converge into an exercise in the co-construction of knowledge.

Scott (2005) points out that in this environment managers are 'able to "play" the dialectic between the top-down, and essentially political, forces of divergence and the "bottom-up" essentially intellectual forces of convergence' (p. 58). Managers have an interest in linking research and teaching for a number of reasons: it is the basis of their academic authority – to establish standards and to self-accredit (or to be accredited by an agency), it helps to attract a high-quality academic workforce, and it is a key to institutional reputation and positioning in the higher education system.

Academics clearly need to navigate the contradictory and ambiguous messages about the relationship between teaching and research. This is important given that the majority of academics occupy positions where they are required to engage in both teaching and research and to do so in a coherent way. One approach that at the time received widespread attention is that of Boyer (1990) and his colleagues, to which we now turn.

Scholarship as the Mediating Link

As noted earlier, Hughes (2005) regards as myth the idea that scholarship is separate from research and teaching, and in doing so he implies that it is central to understanding both teaching and research. The approach of Boyer (1990), working with colleagues in the Carnegie Foundation for the Advancement of Teaching, appeals to universities to 'break out of the tired old teaching versus research debate and define in more creative ways, what it means to be a scholar'. He saw the key academic activities of research, teaching and scholarship as part of a single undertaking, and they moved to distinguish between four types of scholarship:

- The scholarship of discovery – which has to do with increasing the stock of knowledge

- The scholarship of integration – which has to do with making inter-disciplinary connections, making novel interpretations, and coming up with new ideas

- The scholarship of application – which has to do with how know-ledge is applied in the wider community and the mutual interaction between theory and its application

- The scholarship of teaching – which has to do with a particular scholarly approach to teaching that encourages critical and creative thinkers.

This has been a useful distinction for academics because it draws attention to the possibility of developing an approach to teaching and learning that brings it closer to the idea of research. A fruitful approach then, to linking teaching and research, is to teach in a way that emphasises the interactive nature of the relationship, and in a way which promotes a critical orienta-tion that is evident in the best research. Since Boyer there has been a great deal of work on fleshing out what the scholarship of teaching might entail. One common interpretation is encapsulated in various terms such as 'research-led teaching', 'research-enhanced teaching' and 'research-intensive teaching'. Brew (2006) collected examples of what academics understood by the term 'research-led' teaching and was able to classify them into three categories in order of their frequency:

- Learning through research – where students engage in research activities

- Presenting research to students – where research findings are dis-seminated to students

- Researching teaching – where academics conduct research into their own teaching.

The first of these 'learning through research' includes a range of activities such as problem-based learning, group collaborative projects and formal research undertakings. The shift in emphasis from a pedagogy of 'teaching' to a pedagogy of 'learning' has assisted in this respect, since this shift is accompanied by a focus on the use of a wide range of information sources and managing those as a researcher investigating 'real world' problems. The focus on learning has also been associated with a pedagogy of dis-covery and the formation of research-related attributes such as autonomy, independence, critical thinking, creativity and disciplined enquiry. The second understanding of research-led teaching is that teaching is informed by research. This of course is a fairly conventional view: that research increases the stock of knowledge which is then transmitted to students. But this is not what is really meant by the integration of research and teaching. The real issue is the extent to which teachers draw on their own research for teaching, either directly or indirectly. A direct link would be where teachers use their research publications and projects as part of the course content. An indirect link would be where teachers' research provides better frameworks from which to understand particular fields or disciplinary areas: frameworks which suggest a certain line of questioning or a particular set of learning activities. The third understanding above is elaborated by Brew (2006):

> Boyer set out to broaden the notion of scholarship, but one of the effects of his new definitions, particularly the concept of the scholarship of teaching and learning as it has now become known, has been to broaden the nature of what is understood by teaching . . .

> Teaching becomes not just about how these students are going to learn this particular content knowledge, but how the teacher can most effectively engage students in the learning process. In other words teaching becomes in and of itself a form of enquiry. . . . teaching, without a scholarly approach, stagnates. (pp. 98–99)

As such teaching has been reconfigured as lying within a research space – teachers too are like knowledge workers in the new knowledge economy, generating 'working knowledge' from their everyday practice. Of course academics also engage in more formal research on teaching and this has been encouraged by government agencies through the provision of various grants to investigate and improve learning outcomes (irrespective of the disciplinary area of the investigators).

Brew (2006) also makes the point that most studies of the teaching–research relationship look at the way research influences teaching and not the other way around. She then explores the notion of 'teaching-enhanced research' – the various ways in which teaching may benefit research. For example, when ideas for research come from the practice of teaching, or where students undertake pilot research projects that suggest other research projects, when teachers come across new ideas for research as a result of responding to students' questions or as a consequence of preparing a lesson, or when teaching helps to explain the outcomes of research more clearly so that publications are improved and so on. In this connection it should be noted that the diversity of the student body means that teachers are asked a variety of different questions from a variety of viewpoints and this can have benefits for the teacher's understanding of their area of research.

In summary, the idea of the 'scholarship of teaching' can be seen as a mediating link between teaching and research in a number of ways: using research as a pedagogical tool; ensuring that teaching is informed by research, including one's own research; and regarding teaching itself as a form of research enquiry. But what has been neglected in the literature is the 'scholarship of integration' which has to do with the promotion of interdisciplinary connections, new ideas and novel interpretations. This describes quite nicely what is meant by 'innovation'. In a recent enquiry into the national innovation system in Australia (*Venturous Australia: Building strength through innovation*, 2008), Cutler remarks:

> Innovation is commonly described as 'creating value by doing things differently' or 'creating value through doing something in a novel way'. A simple version is 'good ideas put to work' . . . Thus we can describe innovating and being innovative as the process of creative problem solving or solution seeking – designed to produce practical outcomes. The outcome of these processes is the introduction of novel solutions to real problems, needs or opportunities. (p. 15)

Thus innovation is not restricted to the domain of science and technology, and it is much more than simply invention or the application of research to 'real world' problems. As such innovation too can be harnessed as a pedagogical tool through teachers encouraging students to take risks and to think creatively and in novel ways. In a sense the scholarship of teaching can incorporate the scholarship of integration (understood here as innovation), just as it can incorporate the other two scholarships.

Concluding Remarks

It is highly likely that the debate about the relationship between teaching and research will continue to be a feature of academic life – irrespective of any empirical findings that may shed light on the relationship. This is largely because of the ongoing existence of two tendencies: a general political policy and organisation tendency to separate out the two for the purposes of decision making and resourcing; and a contrary tendency to bring together research and teaching in the interests of individual career trajectories and institutional reputations. In this ambiguous and hybrid space individual academics can take heart that there is an intellectual impulse that brings them together as two aspects of a common endeavour: scholarship.

Enhancing Professional Practice

Collect examples of assessments used in a sample of five courses. In what ways do the assessments develop the research attributes of students? How can the assessment items be rewritten to bring out all aspects of what we mean by 'research-led teaching'?

References

Adelman, C. (2008). *The Bologna Club: What U.S. higher education can learn from a decade of European reconstruction.* Washington, DC: Institute for Higher Education Policy.

Aitchison, C., & Lee, A. (2006). Research writing: Problems and pedagogies. *Teaching in Higher Education,* 11(3), 265–278.

Alheit, P., & Dausien, B. (2002). The 'double face' of lifelong learning: Two analytical perspectives on a silent revolution. *Studies in the Education of Adults,* 34(1), 3–22.

Allen Group (2000). *Training to compete: The training needs of industry.* Sydney: Australian Industry Group.

Allen, I. E., & Seaman, J. (2008, November). *Staying the course: Online education in the United States, 2008.* Retrieved from http://www.sloan-c.org.

Anderson, D., Johnson, R., & Saha, L. (2002). *Changes in academic work: Implications for universities of the changing age distribution and work roles of academic staff.* Canberra: DEST.

Andresen, L. (2000). A useable, trans-disciplinary conception of scholarship. *Higher Education Research and Development,* 19(2), 137–153.

Arbogast, W. (2008, April 4). IT on the campuses: What the future holds. *The Chronicle of Higher Education,* 54(30), B6.

Armstrong, P. F. (1982). The needs meeting ideology in liberal adult education. *The International Journal of Lifelong Education,* 1(4), 293–321.

Arrow, H., Poole, M., Henry, K., Wheelan, S., & Moreland, R. (2004). Time, change and development: The temporal perspective on groups. *Small Group Research,* 35(1), 73–105.

Ashraf, W. (2008). Teaching the Google-eyed YouTube generation. Address at the University of Technology, Sydney, Teaching Forum, November 27.

Ashton, D. N. (2004). The impact of organisational structure and practices on learning in the workplace. *International Journal of Training and Development,* 8(1), 43–53.

Ball, S. (2003). The teacher's soul and the terrors of performativity. *Journal of Education Policy,* 18(2), 215–228.

Ball, S. J., Macrae, S., & Maguire, M. (1999). Inclusive education in universities: Why is it important and how it might be achieved. *International Journal of Inclusive Education,* 3(3), 195–224.

Barnett, R. (2003). *Beyond all reason: Living with ideology in the university.* Buckingham, UK: Open University Press/SRHE.

Barnett, R. (Ed.) (2005). *Reshaping the university: New relationships between research, scholarship and teaching.* New York: SRHE and Open University Press.

Barnett, R. (2006). Graduate attributes in an age of uncertainty. In P. Hager, & S. Holland (Eds.), *Graduate attributes, learning and employability* (pp. 49–66). Dordrecht: Springer.

Beckett, D., & Hager, P. (2002). *Life, work and learning: Practice in postmodernity.* London and New York: Routledge.

Beddows, E. (2008). The methodological issues associated with internet-based research. *International Journal of Emerging Technologies and Society,* 6(2), 124–139.

Bereiter, C., & Scardamalia, M. (1993). *Surpassing ourselves: An inquiry into the nature and implications of expertise.* Chicago: Open Court.

Berliner, D. (1987). In pursuit of the expert pedagogue. *Educational Researcher,* 15, 5–13.

Berliner, D. (1994). Expertise: The wonders of exemplary performance. In J. Mangieri, & C. Block (Eds.), *Creating powerful thinking in teachers and students: Diverse perspectives* (pp. 141–186). New York: Holt, Rinehart & Winston.

Berliner, D. (2001). Learning about and learning from expert teachers. *International Journal of Educational Research,* 35(2001), 463–482.

Berliner, D. (2004). Describing the behaviour and documenting the accomplishments of expert teachers. *Bulletin of Science, Technology and Society,* 24(3), 200–212.

Billett, S. (2001). Learning throughout working life: Interdependencies at work. *Studies in Continuing Education,* 23(1), 19–35.

Billett, S. (2002a). Toward a workplace pedagogy: Guidance, participation, and engagement. *Adult Education Quarterly,* 53(1), 27–43.

Billett, S. (2002b). Critiquing workplace learning discourses: Participation and continuity at work. *Studies in the Education of Adults,* 34(1), 56–67.

Billett, S. (2002c). *Learning in the workplace: Strategies for effective practice.* Sydney: Allen & Unwin.

Billett, S. (2006). Constituting the workplace curriculum. *Journal of Curriculum Studies,* 38(1), 31–48.

Black, P., & Wiliam, D. (1998). Assessment and classroom learning. *Assessment in Education,* 5(1), 7–74.

Bloxham, S., & Boyd, P. (2007). *Developing effective assessment in higher education: A practical guide.* Maidenhead, UK: Open University Press, McGraw-Hill Education.

Boud, D. (1988). *Developing student autonomy in learning.* London: Kogan Page.

Boud, D. (1998). A new focus on workplace learning research. In D. Boud (Ed.), *Current issues and new agendas in workplace learning* (pp. 6–11). Leabrook, S. Aust.: NCVER.

Boud, D. (1999). Situating academic development in professional work: Using peer learning. *International Journal for Academic Development,* 4(1), 3–10.

Boud, D. (2000). Sustainable assessment: Rethinking assessment for the learning society. *Studies in Continuing Education,* 22(2), 151–167.

Boud, D., & Falchikov, N. (2007). Introduction: Assessment for the longer term. In D. Boud, & N. Falchikov (Eds.), *Rethinking assessment in higher education* (pp. 3–13). London: Routledge.

Boud, D., & Solomon, N. (Eds.) (2001). *Work-based learning: A new higher education?* Buckingham, UK: SRHE and Open University Press.

Boud, D., & Tennant, M. (2006). Putting doctoral education to work: Challenges to academic practice. *Higher Education Research and Development,* 25(3), 309–322.

Boud, D., Cressey, P., & Doucherty, P. (Eds.) (2006). *Productive reflection at work: Learning in changing organisations.* London: Routledge.

Boud, D., Keogh, R., & Walker, D. (Eds.) (1985). *Reflection: Turning experience into learning.* London: Kogan Page.

Bourdieu, P. (1977). *Outline of a theory of practice* (trans. R. Nice). Cambridge: Polity Press.

Bourdieu, P. (1990a). *The logic of practice*. Stanford, CA: Stanford University Press.

Bourdieu, P. (1990b). *In other words: Essays towards a reflexive practice*. Cambridge: Polity Press.

Bourner, T., Bowden, R., & Laing, S. (2001). Professional doctorates in England. *Studies in Higher Education*, 26(1), 65–83.

Boyer, E. (1990). *Scholarship reconsidered: Priorities for the professoriate*. Princeton, NJ: Carnegie Foundation for the Advancement of Teaching.

Brew, A. (2006). *Research and teaching: Beyond the divide*. New York: Palgrave Macmillan.

Brookfield, S. (2005). *The power of critical theory: Liberating adult learning and teaching*. San Francisco: Jossey-Bass.

Brookfield, S. D. (2006). *The skillful teacher*. San Francisco: Jossey-Bass.

Brown, H. (2006). *Graduate enrolment and degrees: 1986 to 2005*. Washington, DC: Council of Graduate Schools, Office of Research and Information Services.

Bruner, J., & Kalmar, D. (1998). Narrative and metanarrative in the construction of self. In M. Ferrari, & R. Sternberg (Eds.), *Self awareness: Its nature and development* (pp. 308–331). New York: Guilford Press.

Byron, E. (2008, November 19). A new odd couple: Google, P&G swap workers to spur innovation. *The Wall Street Journal*, A1.

Carless, D. (2006). Differing perceptions in the feedback process. *Studies in Higher Education*, 31(2), 219–233.

Carnevale, P. (1991). *America and the new economy*. San Francisco: Jossey-Bass.

Chappell, C. (2005). Investigating learning and work. Proceedings of the Fourth International Conference on Researching Work and Learning, Sydney, December 12–14.

Chappell, C., Rhodes, C., Solomon, N., Tennant, M., & Yates, L. (2003). *Reconstructing the lifelong learner: Pedagogy and identity in individual, social and organisational change*. London: Routledge.

Chi, M., Glaser, R., & Farr, M. (1988). *The nature of expertise*. Hillsdale, NJ: Lawrence Erlbaum Associates.

Clarke, A. (2008). *e-Learning skills* (2nd ed.). New York: Palgrave Macmillan.

Coaldrake, P., & Stedman, L. (1999). *Academic work in the twenty-first century*. Canberra: DEETYA.

Connelly, F., & Clandinin, D. (1990). Stories of experience and narrative inquiry. *Educational Researcher*, 19(5), 2–14.

Council of Graduate Schools (2005). *A renewed commitment to graduate education*. Washington, DC: CGS.

Council of Graduate Schools (2008). *PhD completion project*. Washington, DC: Council of Graduate Schools. Retrieved June 15, 2008 from http://www.phdcompletion.org.

Cranton, P. (2006). *Understanding and promoting transformative learning* (2nd ed.). San Francisco: Jossey-Bass.

Cumming, J. (2008). Representing the complexity, diversity and particularity of the doctoral enterprise in Australia. PhD thesis. Canberra: Australian National University.

Cutler, T. (2008). *Venturous Australia: Building strength through innovation*. Melbourne: Cutler and Company.

Davenport, T., & Prusack, L. (1998). *Working knowledge*. Harvard: Harvard Business School Press.

Davis, B. G. (1993). *Tools for teaching: Collaborative learning, group work and study teams*. San Francisco: Jossey-Bass.

DeBolt, D. (2008, November 12). Universities see double-digit increase in online enrollment. *The Chronicle of Higher Education*. Retrieved November 14, 2008 from http://chronicle.com/wiredcampus/article/3457.

Department of Industry, Science and Resources (DISR) (2000). *Report of human dimension working party for the national innovation summit*. Canberra: DISR.

Docherty, P., Boud, D., & Cressey, P. (2006). Lessons and issues for practice and development. In D. Boud, P. Cressey, & P. Docherty (Eds.), *Productive reflection at work* (pp. 193–206). London: Routledge.

Downes, S. (2008). The future of online learning: Ten years on. Retrieved November 28 from http://halfanhour.blogspot.com/2008/11/future-of-online-learning-ten-years-on_16.html.

du Gay, P. (1997). Organizing identity: Making up people at work. In P. du Gay (Ed.), *Production of culture/Cultures of production* (pp. 285–344). London: Sage Publications.

du Gay, P. (2000). Working knowledge: Productive learning at work conference. Keynote address at University of Technology, Sydney, December 10–13.

Dunleavey, P. (2003). *Authoring a PhD: How to plan, draft, write, and finish a doctoral thesis or dissertation.* New York: Palgrave Macmillan.

Eakin, P. (1999). Autobiography and the value structures of ordinary experiences: Marianne Gullestad's everday life philosophers. In R. Josselson, & A. Lieblich (Eds.), *Making meaning of narratives in the narrative study of lives* (pp. 25–43). Thousand Oaks, CA: Sage Publications.

Earle, R. S. (2002). The integration of instructional technology into public education: Promises and challenges. *ET Magazine, 42*(1), 5–13.

Edwards, R. (1997). *Changing places? Flexibility, lifelong learning and a learning society.* London: Routledge.

Edwards, R., & Usher, R. (1996). What stories do I tell now? New times and new narratives. *International Journal of Lifelong Education, 15*(3), 216–229.

Edwards, R., Ranson, S., & Strain, M. (2002). Reflexivity: Towards a theory of lifelong learning. *International Journal of Lifelong Education, 21*(6), 525–536.

Elbaz, F. (1991). Research on teacher's knowledge: The evolution of a discourse. *Journal of Curriculum Studies, 23*(1), 1–19.

Elton, L., & Johnson, B. (2002). *Assessment in universities: A critical review of research.* York: Higher Education Academy.

Engestrom, Y. (2001). Expansive learning at work: Toward an activity theoretical reconceptualization. *Journal of Education and Work, 14*(1), 133–156.

Engestrom, Y., Miettinen, R., & Punamaki, R.-L. (1999). *Perspectives on activity theory.* New York: Cambridge University Press.

Eraut, M. (1994). *Developing professional knowledge and competence.* London: Falmer Press.

Eraut, M. (2004a). Informal learning in the workplace. *Studies in Continuing Education, 26*(2), 247–273.

Eraut, M. (2004b). Transfer of knowledge between education and workplace settings. In H. Rainbird, A. Fuller, & A. Munro (Eds.), *The context of workplace learning,* pp. 201–221. New York: Routledge.

Eraut, M., Maillardet, F., Miller, C., Steadman, S., Ali, A., Blackman, C., & Furner, J. (2004). *Learning in the first three years of postgraduate Employment.* Annual report to ESRC/TLRP. Brighton: University of Sussex.

Evans, T. (2002). Part-time research students: Are they producing knowledge where it counts? *Higher Education Research and Development, 21*(2), 155–165.

Exley, K., & Dennick, R. (2004). *Small group teaching: Tutorials, seminars and beyond.* London: RoutledgeFalmer.

Fine, P. (2008). *University World News,* Issue 52. Retrieved November 9, 2008 from http://www.universityworldnews.com.

Finn, J. (2005). *Getting a PhD: An action plan to help manage your research, your supervisor and your project.* New York: RoutledgeFalmer.

Fogg, P. (2008, June 6). When your in box is always full. *The Chronicle of Higher Education, 54*(39), B19.

Fraser, R., & Mathews, A. (1999). An evaluation of the desirable characteristics of a supervisor. *Australian Universities' Review, 42*(1), 5–7.

Fry, H., Ketteridge, S., & Marshall, S. (Eds.) (2003). *A handbook for teaching and learning in higher education.* London: Kogan Page.

Fuller, A., & Unwin, L. (1998). Reconceptualising apprenticeship: Exploring the relationship between work and learning. *Journal of Vocational Education and Training, 50*(2), 153–171.

Fuller, A., & Unwin, L. (2002). Developing pedagogies for the contemporary workplace. In K. Evans, P. Hodkinson, & L. Unwin (Eds.), *Working to learn: Transforming learning in the workplace* (pp. 95–111). London: Kogan Page.

Gibbons, M., Limoges, C., Nowotny, H., Schwartzmann, S., Scott, P., & Trow, M. (1994). *The new production of knowledge: The dynamics of science and research in contemporary societies.* London: Sage.

Giddens, A. (1991). *Modernity and self-identity.* Stanford, CA: Stanford University Press.

Goldberger, M., Maher, B., & Flattau, P. (Eds.) (1995). *Research-doctoral programs in the United States: Continuity and change.* Washington: National Academy Press.

Graduate Careers Council Australia (GCA) (2007). *Course experience and graduate destination survey.* Melbourne: GCA.

Griffin, C. (1983). *Curriculum theory in adult and lifelong education.* London: Croom Helm.

Griffiths, S. (1999). Teaching and learning in small groups. In H. Fry, S. Ketteridge, & S. Marshall (Eds.), *A handbook for teaching and learning in higher education* (pp. 91–104). London: Kogan Page.

Griffiths, T. (2004). *New approaches to work experience, new perspectives for learning – Briefing Paper 3.* Brussels: European Commission.

Gurr, G. (2001). Negotiating the 'rackety bridge' – a dynamic model for aligning supervisory style with research student development. *Higher Education Research and Development,* 20(1), 81–92.

Hager, P. (2004). Conceptions of learning and understanding learning at work. *Studies in Continuing Education,* 26(1), 3–17.

Haggis, T. (2006). Pedagogies for diversity: Retaining critical challenge amidst fears of 'dumbing down'. *Studies in Higher Education,* 31(5), 521–535.

Hall, S. (1996). Introduction: Who needs identity? In S. Hall, & P. du Gay (Eds.), *Questions of cultural identity* (pp. 1–17). London: Sage Publications.

Hargreaves, A. (1994). *Changing teachers, changing times: Teachers' work and culture in the postmodern age.* London: Cassell.

Hargreaves, A. (1998). The emotional practice of teaching. *Teaching and Teacher Education,* 14(8), 835–854.

Harman, G. (2002). Producing PhD graduates in Australia for the knowledge economy. *Higher Education Research and Development,* 21(2), 179–190.

Hattie, J., & Marsh, H. (1996). The relationship between research and teaching: A meta-analysis. *Review of Educational Research,* 66(4), 507–542.

Hazelkorn, E. (2007). Consumer concept becomes a policy instrument. *University World News.* Retrieved November 11, 2008 from http://www.universityworldnews.com.

Higgins, R., Hartley, P., & Skelton, A. (2001). Getting the message across: The problem of communicating assessment feedback. *Teaching in Higher Education,* 6(2), 269–274.

Higgs, J., Titchen, A., & Neville, V. (2001). Professional practice and knowledge. In J. Higgs, & A. Titchen (Eds.), *Practice knowledge and expertise in the health professions* (pp. 3–9). Oxford: Butterworth-Heinemann.

Higher Education Academy (HEA) (2007). *National student survey results.* Retrieved June 20, 2007 from http://www.heacademy.ac.uk.

Higher Education Funding Council for England (HEFCE) (2007). Higher Education survey reveals continued student satisfaction, *HEFC News,* 12 September. Retrieved December 13, 2008 from http://www.hefc.ac.uk/news/hefc/2007/nss.htm.

Hochschild, S. (1983). *The managed heart: The commercialization of human feeling.* Berkeley, CA: University of California Press.

Holmes, L. (1999). Competence and capability: From 'confidence trick' to the construction of the graduate identity. In D. O'Reilly, L. Cunningham, & S. Lester (Eds.), *Developing the capable practitioner: Professional capability through higher education* (pp. 83–98). London: Kogan Page.

Horrigan, J. B. (2008, November 16). *When technology fails.* Retrieved November 23, 2008 from http://www.pewinternet.org/index.asp.

Hron, A., & Friedrich, H. (2003). A review of web-based collaborative learning: Factors beyond technology. *Journal of Computer Assisted Learning*, 19, 70–71.

Huddleston, P., & Unwin, L. (2008). *Teaching and learning in higher education: Diversity and change*. London: Routledge.

Hughes, M. (2005). The mythology of research and teaching relationships in universities. In R. Barnett (Ed.), *Reshaping the university: New relationships between research, scholarship and teaching* (pp. 14–26). New York: SRHE and Open University Press.

Ives, G., & Rowley, G. (2005). Supervisor selection or allocation and continuity of supervision: PhD students' progress and outcomes. *Studies in Higher Education*, 30(5), 535–555.

James, R., McInnes, C., & Devlin, M. (2002). *Assessing learning in Australian universities: Ideas, strategies and resources for quality in student assessment*. Melbourne: Centre for the Study of Higher Education, University of Melbourne.

Jan, T. (2008, November 11). Harvard looks to tighten its belt. *The Boston Globe*. Retrieved July 1, 2009 from http://www.boston.com/news/education/higher/articles/2008/11/11/harvard_looks_to_tighten_its_belt/?page=full.

Jaques, D., & Salmon, G. (2007). *Learning in groups: A handbook for face-to-face and online environments* (4th ed.). London: Routledge.

Jensen, T., & Westenholz, A. (Eds.) (2004). *Identity in the age of the new economy: Life in temporary and scattered work practices*. Cheltenham, UK.: Edward Elgar.

Johnson, L., Lee, A., & Green, B. (2000). The PhD and the autonomous self: Gender, rationality and postgraduate pedagogy. *Studies in Higher Education*, 25(2), 135–147.

Johnston, D. (2000). *The new economy*. Paris: OECD.

Kaczynski, D., Wood, L., & Harding, A. (2008). Using radar charts with qualitative evaluation: Techniques to assess change in blended learning. *Active Learning in Higher Education*, 9(1), 23–41.

Karparti, A. (Ed.) (2004). *Promoting equity through ICT in education: Projects, problems, prospects*. Paris: OECD.

Kearns, P. (2001). *Review of research: Generic skills for the new economy*. Leabrook, S. Aust.: NCVER.

Kehm, B. (2004). Developing doctoral degrees and qualifications in Europe: Good practice and issues of concern – a comparative analysis. In J. Sadlak (Ed.), *Doctoral studies and qualifications in Europe and the United States: Status and prospects* (pp. 279–298). Bucharest: UNESCO.

Kemmis, S. (2005). Knowing practice: Searching for saliences. *Pedagogy, Culture and Society*, 13(3), 391–426.

King, R. (2004). *The university in the global age*. London: Palgrave Macmillan.

Knight, P. T., & Yorke, M. (2003). *Assessment, learning and employability*. Maidenhead, UK: Open University Press, McGraw-Hill Education.

Knight, T. (2007). Grading, classifying and future learning. In D. Boud, & N. Falchikov (Eds.), *Rethinking assessment in higher education* (pp. 72–86). London: Routledge.

Latona, C., & Browne, M. (2001). *Some factors associated with completion of research higher degrees*. Canberra: DEST.

Lave, J., & Wenger, E. (1991). *Situated learning: Legitimate peripheral participation*. Cambridge: Cambridge University Press.

Lawson, K. (1975). *Philosophical concepts and values in adult education*. Nottingham: University of Nottingham.

Lea, M. V. (2004). Academic literacies: A pedagogy for course design. *Studies in Higher Education*, 29(6), 739–756.

Lea, M. V., & Street, B. V. (2006). The 'academic literacies' model: Theory and application. *Theory into Practice*, 45(4), 368–377.

Lee, A., & Boud, D. (2003). Writing groups, change and academic identity: Research development as local practice. *Studies in Higher Education*, 28(2), 187–200.

Lemerle, J. (2004). France. In J. Sadlak (Ed.), *Doctoral studies and qualifications in Europe and the United States: Status and prospects* (pp. 37–50). Bucharest: UNESCO.

Lewin, K. (1951). *Field theory in social science.* New York: Harper.

Light, G., & Cox, R. (2001). *Learning & teaching in higher education: The reflective professional.* London: Sage Publications.

Lokken, F., Womer, L., & Mullins, C. (2008, April) *2007 Distance education survey results: Tracking the impact of e-Learning at community colleges.* Retrieved from http://www.itcnetwork.org.

Luft, J. (2000). Insight by surprise. In K. Taylor, C. Marienau, & M. Fiddler (Eds.), *Developing adult learners* (pp. 137–140). San Francisco: Jossey-Bass.

Lynch, S. (2008, February 14). Happy days: Why PhD students need a helping hand from their supervisors. *Independent.* Retrieved July 1, 2009 from http://www.independent.co.uk/news/education/higher/happy-days-why-phd-students-need-a-helping-hand-from-their-supervisors-781842.html.

MacIntyre, A. (1987). The idea of an educated public. In G. Haydon (Ed.), *Education and values: The Richard Peters lecture* (pp. 15–36). London: Institute of Education, University of London.

Malcolm, A. (1975). *The tyranny of the group.* New Jersey: Adams & Co.

Malcolm, J., & Zukas, M. (2001). Bridging pedagogic gaps: Conceptual discontinuities in higher education. *Teaching in Higher Education,* 6(1), 33–42.

Malcolm, J., & Zukas, M. (2002). Altered states of teacher identity: The impact of scrutiny and regulation on pedagogic thinking and practice. SCUTREA, 32nd Annual Conference, Sterling, July 2–4.

Marginson, S. (1995). Markets in higher education: Australia. In J. Smyth (Ed.), *Academic work: The changing labour process in higher education* (pp. 17–39). Buckingham, UK: Society for Research into Higher Education and Open University Press.

Marshall, J. (2008). New ranking scheme for universities. *University World News,* Issue 54. Retrieved November 23, 2008 from www.universityworldnews.com.

Marsick, V. J., & Watkins, K. E. (1990). *Informal and incidental learning in the workplace.* London: Routledge.

McCleod, P. L., & Kettner-Polley, R. B. (2004). Contributions of psychodynamic theories to understanding small groups. *Small Group Research,* 35(3), 333–361.

McCormack, C. (2004). Tensions between student and institutional conceptions of postgraduate research. *Studies in Higher Education,* 29(3), 319–334.

McIntyre, J., & Solomon, N. (2000). The policy environment of work-based learning: globalization, institutions and workplaces. In C. Symes, & J. McIntyre (Eds.), *Working knowledge: The new vocationalism and higher education* (pp. 123–134). Milton Keynes, UK: Open University Press.

McLoughlin, C., & Lee, M. (2007). Social software and participatory learning: Pedagogical choices with technology affordances in the Web 2.0 era. ICT: 'Providing choices for learners and learning'. Proceedings of the Ascilite Conference, Singapore, December 2–5.

McMullen, C. (2008). Developing and sustaining university teaching expertise in times of change: A narrative study with award winning university teachers. Doctoral dissertation, University of Technology, Sydney.

McNamee, S. (1996). Therapy and identity construction in a postmodern world. In D. Grodin, & T. R. Lindlof (Eds.), *Constructing the self in a mediated world* (pp. 141–155). Thousand Oaks, CA: Sage Publications.

McWhinney, W., & Markos, L. (2003). Transformative education: Across the threshold. *Journal of Transformative Education,* 1(1), 16–37.

McWilliam, E., & James, R. (2002). Doctoral education in a knowledge economy. *Higher Education Research and Development,* 21(2), 1.

McWilliam, E., Singh, P., & Taylor, P. (2002). Doctoral education, danger and risk management. *Higher Education Research and Development,* 21(2), 119–129.

Meyer, K. A. (2008). Online program capacity limited, static, elastic, or infinite? *Planning for Higher Education,* 36(2), 54–65.

Miller, A. H., Imrie, B. W., & Cox, K. (1998). *Student assessment in higher education: A handbook for assessing performance.* London: Kogan Page.

Miniwatts Marketing Group (2008, June 30). *World internet users and population stats.* Retrieved August 6, 2008 from http://www.internetworldstats.com/stats.htm.

Mutch, A. (2003). Formative assessment: Revisiting the territory. *Active Learning in Higher Education,* 4(1), 24–38.

Naidoo, R. (2005). Universities in the marketplace: The distortion of teaching and research. In R. Barnett (Ed.), *Reshaping the university: New relationships between research, scholarship and teaching* (pp. 27–36). New York: SRHE and Open University Press.

Nerad, M. (2006). Globalization and its impact on research education: Trends and emerging best practices for the doctorate of the future. In M. Kiley, & G. Mullins (Eds.), *Quality in postgraduate research: Knowledge creation in testing times* (pp. 5–12). Canberra: ANU.

Newman, J. H. (1999). *The idea of a university.* Washington, DC: Regnery Gateway Publishing.

Nias, J. (1996). Thinking about feeling: The emotions in teaching. *Cambridge Journal of Education,* 26(3), 293–306.

Nicol, D., & Macfarlane-Dick, D. (2006). Formative assessment and self-regulated learning: A model and seven principles of good feedback practice. *Studies in Higher Education,* 31(2), 199–218.

Nicoll, K., & Harrison, R. (2003). Constructing the good teacher in higher education: The discursive work of standards. *Studies in Continuing Education,* 25(1), 23–35.

Nixon, J. (1996). Professional identity and the restructuring of higher education. *Studies in Higher Education,* 21(1), 5–16.

Noddings, N. (1984). *Caring: A feminine approach to ethics and moral education.* Berkeley, CA: University of California Press.

Noddings, N. (2003). Is teaching a practice? *The Journal of the Philosophy of Education,* 37(2), 241–251.

Northedge, A. (2003a). Rethinking teaching in the context of diversity. *Teaching in Higher Education,* 8(1), 17–32.

Northedge, A. (2003b). Enabling participation in academic discourse. *Teaching in Higher Education,* 8(2), 169–180.

Nunan, T. E., George, R., & McCausland, H. (2000). Inclusive education in universities: Why is it important and how it might be achieved. *International Journal of Inclusive Education,* 4(1), 63–88.

Nuthall, K. (2008). Massive growth in private tertiary sector. *University World News.* Retrieved May 25, 2008 from http://www.universityworldnews.com.

Olson, J. (1992). *Understanding teaching: Beyond expertise.* Buckingham, UK: Open University Press.

Organisation for Economic Co-operation and Development (OECD) (1994). *Education in a new international setting: Curriculum development for internationalisation – guidelines for country case study.* Paris: OECD.

Organisation for Economic Co-operation and Development (OECD) (1996). *Lifelong learning for all.* Paris: OECD.

Organisation for Economic Co-operation and Development (OECD) (2000). *Is there a new economy? First report of the OECD Growth Project.* Paris: OECD.

Organisation for Economic Co-operation and Development (OECD) (2001). *Investing in competencies for all.* Paris: OECD.

Organisation for Economic Co-operation and Development (OECD) (2003). *The definition and selection of key competencies: Executive summary.* Paris: OECD.

Organisation for Economic Co-operation and Development (OECD) (2007). *Education at a glance 2007: OECD indicators.* Paris: OECD.

Pearson, M. (1999). The changing environment for doctoral education in Australia: Implications for quality management, improvement and innovation. *Higher Education Research and Development,* 18(3), 269–288.

Phillips, E., & Pugh, D. S. (2000). *How to get a PhD: A handbook for students and their supervisors.* Buckingham, UK: Open University Press.

Polanyi, M. (1962). *Personal knowledge: Towards a post-critical philosophy.* London: Routledge & Kegan Paul.

Poole, M., Hollingshead, A., McGrath, J., Moreland, R., & Rohrbaugh, J. (2004). Interdisciplinary perspectives on small groups. *Small Group Research,* 35(1), 3–16.

Pratt, D., & Nesbit, T. (2000). Discourses and cultures of teaching. In A. Wilson, & E. Hayes (Eds.), *Handbook of adult and continuing education* (pp. 117–131). San Francisco: Jossey-Bass.

Prerau, D., Adler, M., & Gunderson, A. (1992). Eliciting and using experiential knowledge and general expertise. In R. Hoffmann (Ed.), *The psychology of expertise: Cognitive research and empirical artificial intelligence* (pp. 99–120). London: Lawrence Erlbaum.

Quality Assurance Agency for Higher Education (QAAHE) (2004). *Code of practice for the assurance of academic quality and standards in higher education. Section 1 Postgraduate research programmes, UK* (pp. 1–39). Mansfield, UK: QAAHE.

Quality Assurance Agency for Higher Education (QAAHE) (2007). *Report on the review of research degree programmes: England and Northern Ireland.* Mansfield, UK: QAAHE.

Rainbird, H., Fuller, A., & Munro, A. (Eds.) (2004). *The context of workplace learning.* New York: Routledge.

Ramsden, P., & Moses, I. (1992). Association between research and teaching in Australian higher education. *Higher Education,* 23, 273–295.

Reynolds, M., & Trehan, K. (2000). Formative assessment and self-regulated learning: A model and seven principles of good feedback practice. *Studies in Higher Education,* 25(3), 267–278.

Richardson, I. (2001). Getting personal: Writing stories. *Qualitative Studies in Education,* 14(1), 33–38.

Rizvi, F., & Walsh, L. (1998). Difference, globalisation and the internationalisation of curriculum. *Australian Universities Review,* 41(2), 7–11.

Rogers, C. (1983). *Freedom to learn for the 1980s.* Columbus, OH: Merrill.

Rose, N. (1996). *Inventing our selves: Psychology, power and personhood.* Cambridge: Cambridge University Press.

Rugg, G., & Petre, M. (2004). *The unwritten rules of PhD research.* Maidenhead, UK: Open University Press.

Rushton, J., Murray, H., & Paunonen, S. (1983). Personlaity, research creativity, and teaching effectiveness in university professors. *Scientometrics,* 5, 93–116.

Ryan, Y. (2004). Teaching and learning in the global era. In R. King (Ed.), *The university in the global age* (pp. 164–180). London: Palgrave Macmillan.

Rychen, D. S., & Salganik, L. H. (Eds.) (2003). *Key competencies for a successful life and a well-functioning society.* Göttingen: Hogrefe & Huber Publishers.

Sadlak, J. (Ed.) (2004). *Doctoral studies and qualifications in Europe and the United States: Status and prospects.* Bucharest: UNESCO.

Sadler, D. R. (1998). Formative assessment: Revisiting the territory. *Assessment in Education,* 5(1), 77–84.

Salmon, G. (2003). *E-moderating: The key to teaching and learning online* (2nd ed.). New York: RoutledgeFalmer.

Sambell, K., McDowell, L., & Sambell, A. (2006). Supporting diverse students: Developing learner autonomy via assessment. In C. Bryan, C. Clegg, & K. Clegg (Eds.), *Innovative assessment in higher education* (pp. 158–168). London: Routledge.

Sarup, M. (1996). *Identity, culture and the postmodern world.* Edinburgh: Edinburgh University Press.

Schön, D. A. (1983). *The reflective practitioner: How professionals think in action.* New York: Basic Books.

Schön, D. A. (1987). *Educating the reflective practitioner.* San Francisco: Jossey-Bass.

Schön, D. A. (1995). Knowing-in-Action: The new scholarship requires a new epistemology. *Change,* November–December, 27–34.

Schön, D. A. (Ed.) (1991). *The reflective turn: Case studies in and on educational practice.* New York: Teachers College Press.

Scott, P. (2005). Divergence or convergence? The links between teaching and research in mass higher education. In R. Barnett (Ed.), *Reshaping the university: New relationships between research, scholarship and teaching* (pp. 53–66). New York: SRHE and Open University Press.

Secretary of State for Trade and Industry (1998). *Our competitive future: Building the knowledge driven economy.* London: DTI.

Shotter, J. (1989). Social accountability and the social construction of 'you'. In J. Shotter, & K. Gergen (Eds.), *Texts of identity* (pp. 131–151). London: Sage Publications.

Shulman, L. (1993). Teaching as community property. *Change,* 25(6), 6–7.

Skelton, A. (1999). An inclusive higher education? Gay and bisexual male teachers and the cultural politics of sexuality. *International Journal of Inclusive Education,* 3(3), 239–255.

Skelton, A. (2004). Understanding 'teaching excellence' in higher education: A critical evaluation of the National Teaching Fellowships Scheme. *Studies in Higher Education,* 29(4), 451–468.

Skelton, A. (2005). *Understanding teaching excellence in higher education: Towards a critical approach.* London: Routledge.

Skule, S., & Reichborn, A. N. (2002). *Learning-conducive work: A survey of learning conditions in Norwegian workplaces.* Luxembourg: CEDEFOP.

Solomon, N. (2008). Interdisciplinary workings: A story to tell. Seminar presented by the Centre for Research in Learning and Change, University of Technology, Sydney, June 5.

Spellings, M. (2006). *A test of leadership: Charting the future of U.S. higher education.* Washington, DC: U.S. Department of Education, Commission on the Future of Higher Education.

Spencer, D. (2008). Widening participation debate heats up. *University World News,* Issue 47. Retrieved October 5, 2008 from www.universityworldnews.com.

Sternberg, D. (1981). *How to complete and survive a doctoral dissertation.* New York: St. Martin's Press.

Sternberg, R. J. (1990). Intelligence and adult learning. Papers from a seminar sponsored by the Center for Adult Learning Research, Montana State University.

Symes, C. (2000). 'Real world' education: The vocationalization of the university. In C. Symes, & J. McIntyre (Eds.), *Working knowledge: The new vocationalism in higher education* (pp. 30–46). Buckingham, UK: Open University Press.

Syverson, M. A., & Slatin, J. (2006). *Evaluating learning in virtual environments.* Retrieved September 2, 2008 from http://www.cwrl.utexas.edu/~Syverson/olr/caeti.html.

Tan, K. (2007). Conceptions of self-assessment: What is needed for long-term learning. In D. Boud, & N. Falchikov (Eds.), *Rethinking assessment in higher education* (pp. 114–127). London: Routledge.

Tennant, M. (1985). The concept of 'need' in adult education. *Australian Journal of Adult Education,* 25(2), 8–12.

Tennant, M. (1998). Adult education as a technology of the self. *International Journal of Lifelong Education,* 13, 364–376.

Tennant, M. (2000) Learning to work, working to learn: Theories of situational education. In C. Symes, & J. McIntyre (Eds.), *Working knowledge: The new vocationalism and higher education* (pp. 123–134). Milton Keynes, UK: Open University Press.

Tennant, M. (2004). Doctoring the knowledge worker. *Studies in Continuing Education,* 26(2), 432–441.

Tennant, M. (2005). Transforming selves. *Journal of Transformative Education,* 3(2), 102–115.

Tennant, M. (2006). *Psychology and adult learning* (3rd ed.). London: Routledge.

Tennant, M. (2009). Regulatory regimes in doctoral education. In D. Boud, & A. Lee (Eds.), *Changing practices of doctoral education* (pp. 226–235). London: Routledge.

Tennant, M., & Roberts, S. (2007). Agreeing to supervise. In C. Denholm, & T. Evans (Eds.), *Supervising doctorates downunder: Keys to effective supervision in Australia and New Zealand* (pp. 20–27). Melbourne: ACER Press.

The College Report (2008). *National survey of student engagement.* Retrieved May 25, 2008 from http://nsse.iub.edu/html/survey_instruments_2008.cfm.

The New Media Consortium and Educause (2008). *Horizon report. The new media consortium and educause learning initiative.* Stanford, CA: New Media Consortium.

Thomas, D. (Ed.) (1995). *Teachers' stories.* Buckingham, UK: Open University Press.

Timma, H. (2005). Performative assessment and worker identity(ies). Proceedings of 14th National Vocational Education and Research Conference, Wodonga.

Timma, H. (2007). Experiencing the workplace: Sharing worker identities through assessment, work and learning. *Studies in Continuing Education,* 29(2), 163–179.

Tom, A. (1997). The deliberative relationship: A frame for talking about faculty-student relationships. *The Alberta Journal of Educational Research,* 43(1), 3–21.

Townsend, B. K., & Rosser, V. J. (2007). Workload issues and measures of faculty productivity. *The NEA Higher Education Journal: Thought & Action,* 23, 7–20.

Tuckman, B., & Jensen, M. (1977). Stages of small group development. *Group and Organisational Studies,* 2, 419–427.

Usher, R. (2000). Imposing structure, enabling play: New knowledge production and the 'real world' university. In C. Symes, & J. McIntyre, (Eds.), *Working knowledge: The new vocationalism and higher education* (pp. 98–110). Milton Keynes, UK: Open University Press.

Usher, R. (2002). A diversity of doctorates: Fitness for the knowledge economy? *Higher Education Research and Development,* 21(2), 143–153.

Van Manen, M. (1997). *Researching lived experience: Human science for an action sensitive pedagogy* (2nd ed.). London, Ont.: Althouse Press.

Vilkinas, T. (1998). Management of the Phd process: The challenging role of the supervisor. In M. Kiley, & G. Mullins (Eds.), *Quality in postgraduate research: Managing the new agenda.* Adelaide: University of Adelaide.

Weigel, R. G. (2002). The marathon encounter group-vision and reality: Exhuming the body for a last look. *Counseling Psychology Journal: Practice and Research,* 54, 186–298.

Welch, J. (2001, September 29). CEOs just want to have fun in the 'real game'. *Sydney Morning Herald,* p. 1.

Wenger, E. (1998). *Communities of practice: Learning, meaning and identity.* Cambridge: Cambridge University Press.

Wiltshire, H. (1973). The concepts of learning and need in adult education. *Studies in Adult Education,* 5(1), 26–30.

Winter, R., Griffiths, M., & Green, K. (2000). The 'academic' qualities of practice: What are the criteria for a practice-based PhD? *Studies in Higher Education,* 25(1), 25–37.

Yeatman, A. (1995). Making supervision relationships accountable: Graduate student logs. *Australian Universities' Review,* 38(2), 9–11.

Yorke, M. (2003). Formative assessment in higher education: Moves towards theory and the enhancement of pedagogic practice. *Higher Education,* 45, 477–501.

Zeichner, K., & Liston, D. (1987). Teaching student teachers to reflect. *Harvard Educational Review,* 57(1), 23–48.

Index